TEXAS
WRITE
SOURCE

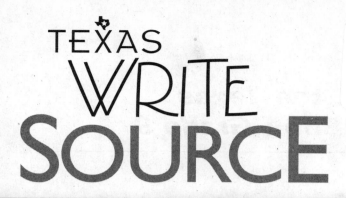

SkillsBook

Grade 9

GREAT SOURCE.

HOUGHTON MIFFLIN HARCOURT

MW00995908

A Few Words About the *Texas Write Source SkillsBook* Grade 9

Before you begin . . .

The *SkillsBook* provides you with opportunities to practice the editing and proofreading skills presented in the *Write Source* textbook. The textbook contains guidelines, examples, and models to help you complete your work in the *SkillsBook*.

Each *SkillsBook* activity includes a brief introduction to the topic and refers you to the pages in the textbook that offer additional information and examples. The "Proofreading Activities" focus mostly on the mechanics of writing. The "Parts of Speech Activities" highlight each of the eight parts of speech. The "Sentence Activities" provide practice in sentence combining and in correcting common sentence problems.

The Extend

Many activities include an **Extend** at the end of the exercise. Its purpose is to provide ideas for follow-up work that will help you apply what you have learned to your own writing.

Copyright © by Houghton Mifflin Harcourt Publishing Company

All rights reserved. No part of this work may be reproduced or transmitted in any form or by any means, electronic or mechanical, including photocopying or recording, or by any information storage or retrieval system, without the prior written permission of the copyright owner unless such copying is expressly permitted by federal copyright law.

Permission is hereby granted to individuals using the corresponding student's textbook or kit as the major vehicle for regular classroom instruction to photocopy entire pages from this publication in classroom quantities for instructional use and not for resale. Requests for information on other matters regarding duplication of this work should be addressed to Houghton Mifflin Harcourt Publishing Company, Attn: Paralegal, 9400 South Park Center Loop, Orlando, Florida 32819.

Printed in the U.S.A.

ISBN-13   978-0-547-39498-5

2 3 4 5 6 7 8 9 10 11 12   0956   19 18 17 16 15 14 13 12 11

4500306118   BCDEFG

If you have received these materials as examination copies free of charge, Houghton Mifflin Harcourt Publishing Company retains title to the materials and they may not be resold. Resale of examination copies is strictly prohibited.

Possession of this publication in print format does not entitle users to convert this publication, or any portion of it, into electronic format.

CONTENTS

Proofreading Activities

Editing for Mechanics

Pretest: Punctuation **3**

END PUNCTUATION

End Punctuation 1 and 2 **5**
Review: End Punctuation 7

COMMAS

Commas Between Independent Clauses **8**
Commas in a Series & Commas to Separate Adjectives 1 and 2 **9**
Commas After Introductory Phrases and Clauses 1 and 2 **11**
Review: Commas 1 13
Commas to Set Off Explanatory Words & Appositives **14**
Commas with Nonrestrictive Phrases and Clauses 1, 2, and 3 **15**
Other Uses for Commas **19**
Review: Commas 2 20

SEMICOLONS & COLONS

Semicolons to Join Independent Clauses **21**
Colons **23**
Review: Semicolons & Colons 24

HYPHENS & DASHES

Hyphens 1 and 2 **25**
Dashes **27**
Review: Hyphens & Dashes 28

APOSTROPHES

Apostrophes in Contractions &
    to Show Omitted Letters or Numbers **29**
Apostrophes to Form Possessives 1 and 2 **30**
Review: Apostrophes 32

© Houghton Mifflin Harcourt Publishing Company

QUOTATION MARKS & ITALICS (UNDERLINING)

Quotation Marks with Titles & Special Words **33**

Quotation Marks with Dialogue **34**

Quotation Marks & Diagonals **35**

Italics (Underlining) & Quotation Marks **36**

Review: Quotation Marks & Italics (Underlining) 37

OTHER FORMS OF PUNCTUATION

Punctuation in Math **38**

Punctuation for Other Needs 1 and 2 **39**

CAPITALIZATION

Pretest: Capitalization **41**

Capitalization 1, 2, and 3 **43**

Review: Capitalization 46

NUMBERS, ABBREVIATIONS, & ACRONYMS

Pretest: Numbers & Abbreviations **47**

Numbers **48**

Abbreviations, Acronyms, & Initialisms **49**

Review: Numbers & Abbreviations 50

PLURALS & SPELLING

Pretest: Plurals & Spelling **51**

Plurals 1 and 2 **52**

Spelling 1 and 2 **54**

Review: Plurals & Spelling 56

Using the Right Word

Pretest: Using the Right Word **57**

Using the Right Word 1, 2, 3, 4, and 5 **58**

Review: Using the Right Word 63

Proofreading Review 65

© Houghton Mifflin Harcourt Publishing Company

Parts of Speech Activities

Nouns

Pretest: Nouns **69**

Classes of Nouns 1 and 2 **70**

Functions of Nouns **72**

Nominative, Possessive, & Objective Cases of Nouns **73**

Review: Nouns 74

Pronouns

Pretest: Pronouns **75**

Types of Pronouns **76**

Personal Pronouns **77**

Number & Person of Personal Pronouns **78**

Functions of Pronouns **79**

Nominative, Possessive, & Objective Cases of Pronouns 1 and 2 **80**

Pronoun Cases: *I* and *Me* **82**

Review: Pronouns 1 83

Reflexive & Intensive Pronouns **84**

Reciprocal Pronouns **85**

Relative Pronouns **86**

Indefinite, Interrogative, & Demonstrative Pronouns **87**

Review: Pronouns 2 88

Verbs

Pretest: Verbs **89**

Types of Verbs **90**

Auxiliary (Helping) & Linking Verbs **91**

Present, Past, & Future Tense Verbs **92**

Perfect Tense Verbs **93**

Review: Verbs 1 94

Active & Passive Voice **95**

Indicative & Imperative Moods **96**

Subjunctive Mood **97**

Transitive & Intransitive Verbs **98**

Direct & Indirect Objects **99**

Verbals: Gerunds, Infinitives, & Participles **100**

Irregular Verbs 1, 2, and 3 **101**

Irregular Verbs: *Lie* and *Lay* **104**

Review: Verbs 2 105

© Houghton Mifflin Harcourt Publishing Company

Adjectives & Adverbs

Pretest: Adjectives & Adverbs **107**
Adjectives **108**
Predicate Adjectives **109**
Forms of Adjectives **110**
Review: Adjectives 111
Adverbs **112**
Types of Adverbs **113**
Forms of Adverbs **114**
Using *Good* and *Well* **115**
Review: Adverbs 116

Prepositions, Conjunctions, & Interjections

Pretest: Prepositions, Conjunctions, & Interjections **117**
Prepositions & Interjections **118**
Coordinating Conjunctions **119**
Correlative Conjunctions **120**
Subordinating Conjunctions **121**
Review: Prepositions, Conjunctions, & Interjections 122

Parts of Speech Review 123

© Houghton Mifflin Harcourt Publishing Company

Sentence Activities

Sentence Basics

SUBJECTS & PREDICATES

Pretest: Subjects & Predicates **127**
Simple Subjects & Predicates **128**
Simple, Complete, & Compound Subjects and Predicates **129**
Review: Subjects & Predicates 130

PHRASES

Pretest: Phrases **131**
Verbal Phrases **132**
Prepositional Phrases **133**
Appositive Phrases **134**
Review: Phrases 135

CLAUSES

Pretest: Clauses **136**
Independent & Dependent Clauses **137**
Adverb, Adjective, & Noun Clauses **138**
Review: Clauses 139
Review: Phrase or Clause? 140

SENTENCE VARIETY

Pretest: Sentences **141**
Basic Sentence Patterns **142**
Kinds of Sentences **143**
Types of Sentences **144**
Modeling a Sentence 1 and 2 **145**
Review: Sentences 147

SUBJECT-VERB AGREEMENT

Pretest: Subject-Verb Agreement **148**
Subject-Verb Agreement 1, 2, and 3 **149**
Review: Subject-Verb Agreement 152

PRONOUN-ANTECEDENT AGREEMENT

Pretest: Pronoun-Antecedent Agreement **153**
Pronoun-Antecedent Agreement 1 and 2 **154**
Review: Pronoun-Antecedent Agreement 156

© Houghton Mifflin Harcourt Publishing Company

Sentence Combining

Pretest: Sentence Combining **157**
Sentence Combining 1 and 2 **159**
Review: Sentence Combining 162

Sentence Problems

COMMA SPLICES & RUN-ON SENTENCES

Pretest: Sentence Problems **163**
Comma Splices & Run-On Sentences 1, 2, and 3 **165**

SENTENCE FRAGMENTS & RAMBLING SENTENCES

Sentence Fragments 1 and 2 **168**
Rambling Sentences **170**
Review: Sentence Problems 1 171

MISPLACED & DANGLING MODIFIERS

Misplaced Modifiers **172**
Dangling Modifiers **173**

WORDINESS & UNPARALLEL CONSTRUCTION

Wordiness & Deadwood **174**
Nonstandard Language **175**
Unparallel Construction 1 and 2 **176**
Review: Sentence Problems 2 179

SHIFTS IN CONSTRUCTION

Pretest: Shifts in Construction **181**
Shifts in Construction **182**
Shifts in Verb Tense 1 and 2 **183**
Pronoun Shifts **185**
Review: Shifts in Construction 186

Sentence Review 187

Posttests for SkillsBook Activities **189**

Posttest Answer Key **235**

© Houghton Mifflin Harcourt Publishing Company

Proofreading Activities

The activities in this section of your *SkillsBook* include sentences that need to be checked for mechanics, including punctuation and capitalization, or correct word choices. Most of the activities also include helpful textbook references. In addition, the **Extend** activities provide follow-up practice of certain skills.

Editing for Mechanics   **3**

Using the Right Word   **57**

Proofreading Review   **65**

© Houghton Mifflin Harcourt Publishing Company

 **TEKS** 9.18B, 9.18B(i), 9.18B(iii)

Pretest: Punctuation

Place periods, commas, and apostrophes where they are needed in the following paragraph.

1 I was new at school, but I wasn't alone. One-fourth of us were new

2 at school. We were ninth graders entering Betsy Ross High School for the

3 2005–2006 school year but I was *really* new because I had just moved to

4 town from Portland Oregon I walked down the long crowded hallways with

5 what I hoped looked like a calm expression but my brain was turning a

6 million miles an hour I was thinking to myself "How am I going to fit

7 in?" I was thinking so hard that I somehow didnt see a huge red-haired

8 guy with a buzz cut He was a real mountain and my head knocked into

9 his left shoulder.

Place dashes, quotation marks, and underlining (for italics) in the following paragraphs.

1 I I'm sorry, I blurted. He rolled his eyes, shook his head, and strolled

2 down the hallway, completely ignoring me.

3 Well, maybe fitting in wasn't even possible among these giants; maybe

4 I should have just been praying that I wouldn't get crushed. Everyone

5 seemed to be much larger at least four inches taller and sixty pounds

6 heavier than I was. Man, oh man, I thought out loud. How big do they

7 grow kids around here? I felt like I was in the middle of a Honey, I

8 Shrunk the Ninth Grader movie.

© Houghton Mifflin Harcourt Publishing Company

Place semicolons, hyphens, and colons where they are needed in the following paragraphs.

1   To make myself feel better, I made a mental list of my talents I

2 could touch my nose with the tip of my tongue I could drink a glass of

3 water while standing on my head and, as an encore, I could sing "The

4 Star Spangled Banner" like Donald Duck. In the smarts department, I

5 knew I wasn't the dullest crayon in the box my grades were B's and C's.

6   Yikes! It was 7 44. I walked casually into the room however, I

7 immediately looked at the front of the room. I didn't want to make eye

8 contact with any of the kids. I wasn't ready. I looked at the blackboard

9 the teacher had written the following letter

Add colons, commas, and quotation marks where they are needed in the following paragraphs.

1   Dear Students

2   My name is Mrs. Bardurian. Look on your schedule and if

3   you do not have P1—English 9—Rm 195 printed on the first line

4   you are in the wrong place.

5   If you are in the right place get out a sheet of paper and

6   tell me about yourself. This is between you and me. Your goal is

7   very simple Find your voice and use it.

8   Sincerely

9   Mrs. Bardurian

10   I thought Find your voice and use it? Sure, if I can stop shaking long

11 enough to find my pen and paper, I'd be happy to look for my voice.

© Houghton Mifflin Harcourt Publishing Company

TEKS 9.18B

End Punctuation 1

The rules for end punctuation are very simple: (1) place a period at the end of a sentence that is a statement, (2) use a question mark if the sentence asks a question, and (3) use an exclamation point to express strong feelings. For more information about end punctuation, turn to 659.1, 660.1, and 660.2 in *Write Source*.

> **Place** periods, question marks, and exclamation points where they are needed in the following paragraphs. Also supply the necessary capital letters.

1   Why do more and more Americans take vitamin supplements? they

2   hope to stop cancer, heart disease, stress, hair loss, and other ailments

3   Americans spend $3.3 billion annually on megavitamins (large-dose

4   vitamins) examples include vitamin C with rose hips, an A-and-D combo,

5   vitamin B complex, selenium, beta-carotene, and zinc daily vitamin

6   supplements are not considered megavitamins

7   some people use a computer program to determine which megavitamins

8   to take they enter their age, sex, and other personal factors into the

9   computer program it calculates their vitamin needs other people follow

10   the guidelines listed in the government's figures for Recommended Dietary

11   Allowances (RDA)

12   what do the experts say about taking megadoses some say megadoses,

13   in certain cases, are beneficial others argue that the benefits of megadose

14   supplements remain largely unproven one thing that everyone agrees upon

15   is that people should try to meet as many of their vitamin and mineral

16   needs as they can by eating a healthful diet megavitamins are not

17   substitutes for good food

Extend: Choose a subject that interests you. Write a paragraph (or two) like the ones above. Leave out all end punctuation and capitalization. Exchange paragraphs with a classmate and add the necessary punctuation and capital letters. Check each other's work.

© Houghton Mifflin Harcourt Publishing Company

TEKS 9.18B
ELPS 5G

End Punctuation 2

End punctuation marks—periods, question marks, and exclamation points—help readers move easily through your writing. For more information about end punctuation, turn to 659, 660.1, and 660.2 in *Write Source*.

Place periods, question marks, and exclamation points where they are needed in the following paragraphs. Also put in capital letters where needed.

1 **M**any people visit Nashville, Tennessee. the wooded, rolling hills and

2 the Cumberland River make Nashville a beautiful city most people come

3 to hear country music, though, and to see their favorite musicians

4 Nashville has long been known as the world's capital of country music

5 can you believe it has more than 90 record labels, about 175 recording

6 studios, and 290 music publishing companies some musicians have their

7 own labels for example, John Prine started Oh Boy! Records, and Steve

8 Earle started E-Squared Records here.

9 Tourist attractions abound in Nashville the Grand Ole Opry Museum

10 draws thousands of people shrines dedicated to famous artists like Hank

11 Williams and Minnie Pearl are also popular tourist spots tour buses cruise

12 past the current and former homes of stars.

13 visitors to Nashville keep their eyes open for a glimpse of a country

14 music star one of the best places to bump into a star is Music Row you

15 are also likely to see famous singers in an ordinary place like the post

16 office, a mall, or a grocery store would you like to visit Nashville and

17 meet a superstar what a thrill that would be

Extend: Write a short piece describing a place you have visited or a place you would like to visit. Include sentences that require periods, question marks, and exclamation points, but don't put in the end punctuation or beginning capitalization. Exchange papers with a classmate and add the correct punctuation and capital letters.

© Houghton Mifflin Harcourt Publishing Company

TEKS 9.18B

Review: End Punctuation

> **Place** periods, question marks, and exclamation points where they are needed in the following article. Also put in capital letters at the beginnings of sentences.

1   The Iditarod, Alaska's famous race for sled-dog teams, begins in

2   Anchorage and ends in Nome. *T*hat's a distance of 1,150 miles the first leg

3   of the race winds through birch forests, crosses frozen lakes, and follows

4   winding rivers soon the trail begins to rise, climbing into the mountains

5   the sleds cross over the range at Rainy Pass, almost 3,200 feet high to the

6   north of Rainy Pass, the mushers can see Mount McKinley (did you know

7   that this is the tallest peak in North America) it is a magnificent sight

8   once out of the mountains, the trail drops into the Interior—a part of

9   Alaska that Jack London called "the land of icy silence" temperatures in

10   the −30's are common there in fact, the mercury may drop to −50°F or

11   even −70°F (how would you survive such cold temperatures) some of the

12   time, the trail follows the Kuskokwim River rolling hills and a few spruce

13   trees alternate with tundra until the trail reaches the Yukon

14   in the Yukon, the icy silence gives way to howling winds these north

15   winds can exceed 50 miles an hour next the trail rises and crosses a low

16   pass in the Nulato Hills before dropping down to the coast many miles

17   of the Iditarod trail lie on the frozen Bering Sea the hard grains of snow

18   scrape the dogs' feet, and shifting ice can hide trail markers

19   The early camaraderie of the race has given way to competition the

20   winner—from more than 70 teams—takes home nearly $100,000 in cash

21   and prizes can you believe these sled-dog teams spend as long as two

22   weeks on the trail in subzero weather

© Houghton Mifflin Harcourt Publishing Company

TEKS 9.18B

Commas Between Independent Clauses

A comma precedes a coordinating conjunction that links two independent clauses. The coordinating conjunctions are *and, but, or, nor, for, so,* and *yet.* You can add variety to your writing by combining independent clauses with a coordinating conjunction and a comma to form compound sentences. Turn to 662.1 in *Write Source.*

Study the sentences below. Place commas before the coordinating conjunctions that join two independent clauses.

1. The pretzel was probably invented in the seventh century by monks, and the children they taught loved the treat.

2. The first pretzels were soft and doughy but today we also eat and enjoy the hard, crispy ones.

3. Hard pretzels may have been invented by a baker who fell asleep so the pretzels he had in the oven baked to a crisp.

4. Water, flour, and yeast are the basic ingredients and often a sprinkling of salt is added to the outside.

5. A long time ago, some brides and grooms used pretzels in their wedding ceremonies for it was believed that pretzels brought good luck.

6. The most popular pretzel shape is the twist but pretzels also come shaped as nuggets, sticks, and rings.

7. A one-ounce serving of pretzels contains approximately 110 calories yet it contains almost no fat.

8. Pretzels continue to be a favorite snack for Americans but potato chips and tortilla chips are still more popular.

9. Do you like pretzels or do you prefer chips?

Extend: Take a closer look at the coordinating conjunctions that connect the independent clauses in the sentences above. Then, on your own paper, write a sentence for each of the seven coordinating conjunctions listed at the top of this page.

© Houghton Mifflin Harcourt Publishing Company

TEKS 9.18B
ELPS 5G

Commas in a Series & Commas to Separate Adjectives 1

Commas separate words, phrases, or clauses in a series. A series must always contain at least three items. Turn to 664.2 in *Write Source* for more information.

> **The Abominable Snowman is said to have a face like a beast, arms like an ape, and legs like a human.**

Commas also separate two or more adjectives that equally modify a noun. Turn to 662.2 in *Write Source* for more information.

> **Legend has it that the Abominable Snowman is a sly, elusive beast that resembles a huge ape.**

Insert commas where needed to separate items in a series in the sentences below. Also insert commas between adjectives that equally modify a noun.

1. This huge, hairy beast is said to walk upright like a human.

2. Reports say such creatures live on the high frigid peaks of the Himalaya Mountains, as well as in remote parts of China Russia and Canada.

3. According to some stories, the Abominable Snowman comes down from the mountains to attack villagers goats and sheep.

4. Since the 1890s, explorers have discovered strange footprints in the cold hard snow.

5. There is no direct reliable evidence that the Abominable Snowman exists.

6. This creature is called a yeti the Abominable Snowman or Bigfoot.

7. Eric Shipton—a respected well-known explorer—took pictures of gigantic tracks in the snow near Mount Everest in 1951.

8. Many explorers went to Mount Everest to see for themselves, but none glimpsed the gigantic hairy apelike creature.

Extend: Write a paragraph about a beast from a book, movie, or your imagination. Use adjectives that equally describe some of your nouns. Use the two tests to determine if your adjectives are equal. (Turn to "A Closer Look" under 662.2 in *Write Source*.)

© Houghton Mifflin Harcourt Publishing Company

★ TEKS 9.18B

Commas in a Series &
Commas to Separate Adjectives 2

Commas separate words, phrases, or clauses in a series. A series must always contain at least three items. Turn to 664.2 in *Write Source* for more information.

> **Stock cars have special engines, doors, and windshields.**

Commas also separate two or more adjectives that equally modify a noun. Turn to 662.2.

> **Stock-car racing is a popular, well-respected spectator sport.**

> **Insert** commas where needed below to separate items in a series. Also insert commas between equal adjectives. Two sentences do not need commas inserted.

1. Stock cars are altered to increase their speed, power, and endurance.

2. Until recently only American-made late-model sedans could be raced.

3. Stock cars look similar to ordinary passenger cars, the kind that car dealers have in stock.

4. Drivers sit in the usual upright position, but they are strapped in with heavy reinforced seat belts and shoulder harnesses.

5. Stock cars are heavier than formula-one cars Indy cars or drag-racing cars.

6. Stock cars have reinforced steel bodies and special fiberglass spoilers.

7. The well-tuned high-power engine in a stock car pushes it to speeds of 190 miles per hour.

8. Race-car drivers prefer fast smooth tracks.

9. Some races are held on super speedways that have wide high-banked corners where cars can make the curves at nearly 175 miles per hour.

10. Racing flags signal drivers to drive with caution to make a pit stop to let a faster car pass or to stop.

Extend: Compose four sentences about cars. In two of the sentences, use equal adjectives; in the other two, include a series of items. Use commas correctly.

© Houghton Mifflin Harcourt Publishing Company

TEKS 9.18B

Commas After Introductory Phrases and Clauses 1

A comma is used to separate an introductory word group from the rest of the sentence. Introductory word groups are usually clauses or phrases. Turn to 662.1 and 664.3 in *Write Source*. Read the examples carefully. By reading a sentence, you will sense when the introductory material ends and the main idea begins, but it is wise to learn to identify phrases and clauses. Turn to 784.1 and 786.

> **Read** each sentence below and insert commas where needed. Three sentences do not need commas.

1. During a long winter with lots of snow, there is no place on earth like the National Elk Refuge in Jackson Hole, Wyoming.

2. From November through April the National Elk Refuge is home to about 7,500 elk.

3. When deep snow makes it hard to find food elk come to this animal preserve.

4. The elk are fed alfalfa pellets to supplement their diet of natural grasses.

5. Prior to the establishment of the refuge many elk starved.

6. Once the elk are safely within the refuge they quickly learn to follow the feed wagon.

7. On their way to the National Elk Refuge the elk face many hunters.

8. Each year hunters kill thousands of elk.

9. Some people feel that hunting is necessary because the ever-growing herd gets too large to be supported by the refuge throughout the winter.

10. Sitting in an open sleigh pulled by a Belgian draft horse visitors can take a 45-minute ride among the elk herd.

11. At the visitor center you can view a slide show, a film, and a number of exhibits about the National Elk Refuge.

Extend: Write three to five sentences using introductory word groups. Tell about visiting a relative's home or about a place you and your friends often visit. Underline your introductory word groups and add commas as needed.

© Houghton Mifflin Harcourt Publishing Company

TEKS 9.18B

Commas After Introductory Phrases and Clauses 2

Introductory word groups, which are usually phrases and clauses, are set off from the rest of the sentence with a comma. Read a sentence carefully. You will sense when the introductory material ends and the main sentence begins. Place a comma at that point. Turn to 662.1 and 664.3 in *Write Source*. Read the examples, pausing at the commas. For information about clauses and phrases, turn to 784.1 and 786.

Place commas after the introductory word groups in the following sentences.

1. Located at the Pacific Ocean's entrance to San Francisco Bay, the Golden Gate Bridge spans 4,600 feet of water.

2. Since the bridge spans the Golden Gate Strait it is called the Golden Gate Bridge.

3. Expecting the bridge to be gold-colored many visitors are surprised to see the bright red-orange color.

4. When selecting the orange color Irving F. Morrow, consulting architect, said he thought the color would enhance the area's natural beauty.

5. As early as 1872 some people started talking about spanning the Golden Gate Strait, especially a railroad entrepreneur named Charles Crocker.

6. Nearly 50 years later the idea of a bridge was revived by James Wilkins, newspaper editor for the *San Francisco Call Bulletin*.

7. Early in the summer of 1921 a cost estimate—$27 million—was presented by Joseph Strauss, an architect.

8. As is often the case when something new is proposed many people, including other architects, criticized the plans.

9. Fortunately for the people of San Francisco the bridge has been used with very few problems for 75 years.

Extend: Write three sentences about another famous structure in the United States. Introduce each sentence with a clause or a phrase and, of course, a comma.

© Houghton Mifflin Harcourt Publishing Company

Review: Commas 1

> **Place** commas in each sentence. Write the rule that explains the use of each comma.

1. Abstract art is a kind of painting, drawing, and sculpture that flourished in the twentieth century.

RULE: *Use commas to separate items in a series.*

2. While traditional painters filled their canvases with objects that a viewer could easily identify abstract artists were likely to fill their canvases with shapes, swirls, and thick paint.

RULE: _____

3. Pablo Picasso Alexander Calder and Henry Moore all created abstract art.

RULE: _____

4. These bold innovative artists rejected many of the rules and customs of earlier art.

RULE: _____

5. To provide contrast in their art some abstract painters left portions of their canvases unpainted.

RULE: _____

6. Jackson Pollock—a free-thinking energetic painter—dripped and splattered paint onto a canvas spread on the floor.

RULE: _____

7. This seemingly carefree undisciplined painting bewildered critics viewers and some artists.

RULE: _____

RULE: _____

8. The critics began to call Pollock and others like him "action painters" but most people today simply refer to them as abstract painters.

RULE: _____

_____

© Houghton Mifflin Harcourt Publishing Company

TEKS 9.18B(ii)

Commas to Set Off Explanatory Words & Appositives

Commas are used to enclose an explanatory word or phrase. Turn to 666.2 in *Write Source*.

> **The Dixie Chicks, a crossover musical group, attracts both country and pop music fans.**

A specific kind of explanatory word or phrase called an *appositive* identifies or renames a preceding noun or pronoun. Turn to 664.1 in *Write Source*.

> **This group has two backup singers to support the lead vocalist, Natalie Maines.**

Place commas where they are needed below.

1. Two sisters, Emily (Erwin) Robison and Martie (Erwin) Seidel, started The Dixie Chicks.

2. They joined with Natalie Maines a pop vocalist in 1995.

3. The sisters Emily and Martie grew up studying classical music.

4. They also played two stringed instruments the fiddle and the banjo.

5. A popular third-party presidential candidate Ross Perot asked them to play at fund-raisers.

6. This candidate Perot was also a successful businessman and was a fan of The Dixie Chicks when they were still a little-known group.

7. Emily Robison and Martie Seidel the two sisters recorded three independent albums before forming the current group.

8. The two young musicians well trained in the basics of music once sang on street corners.

9. The Dixie Chicks a crossover trio have won several Country Music Awards, American Music Awards, and Grammy Awards.

10. This group headquartered in Nashville attracts both country and pop music fans.

Extend: Write three to five sentences about a music group you like. Use explanatory phrases and appositives. Be sure to punctuate your sentences correctly.

© Houghton Mifflin Harcourt Publishing Company

TEKS 9.17A(ii), 9.18B(ii)

Commas with Nonrestrictive Phrases and Clauses 1

Nonrestrictive phrases and clauses, sometimes called unnecessary or nonessential word groups, can be removed from a sentence without changing its basic meaning. Always place commas around nonrestrictive phrases and clauses. Study the examples below and compare nonrestrictive clauses with restrictive clauses. Turn to 666.2 in *Write Source* for more information.

> **Auroras, *which are displays of light in the sky*, can be seen only at night.**
> (nonrestrictive clause)

> **Lights that dance in the night sky are called auroras.**
> (restrictive clause.)

> **Auroras, *flickering lights in the evening sky*, inspire poets.**
> (nonrestrictive phrase)

> **People wanting to see auroras must wait patiently since auroras do not occur every night.** (restrictive phrase)

Place commas around the nonrestrictive phrases and clauses in the sentences below. (Some sentences have no nonrestrictive phrases or clauses.)

1. Auroras, electrically charged particles from the sun, illuminate the sky.

2. The electrically charged particles that travel toward the earth's magnetic field collide with atoms and molecules in our atmosphere.

3. Auroras which are called *aurora borealis* in the northern hemisphere and *aurora australis* in the southern hemisphere move and flicker.

4. People in far northern or southern regions often see the auroras.

5. The colors that are most often seen in auroras are green, red, and purple.

6. Auroras which sometimes extend for thousands of miles across the sky occur from 60 to 620 miles above the earth.

7. The solar wind which carries a continuous stream of electrically charged particles from the sun is the source of auroras.

8. Violent eruptions on the sun increase the number of electrically charged particles that travel into the earth's atmosphere on the solar wind.

Extend: Write four sentences about the sun and the stars. In the first two, include a nonrestrictive phrase or clause. In the other two, include a restrictive phrase or clause.

© Houghton Mifflin Harcourt Publishing Company

⭐ **TEKS** 9.17A(ii), 9.18B(ii)

Commas with Nonrestrictive Phrases and Clauses 2

Nonrestrictive phrases and clauses, also called nonessential or unnecessary word groups, can be removed from a sentence without changing the basic meaning of the sentence. Nonrestrictive phrases and clauses are set off with commas. Turn to 666.2 in *Write Source*.

> **Place** commas around the nonrestrictive phrases and nonrestrictive clauses in the following sentences.

1. New York City subways‚ which run both above and below ground‚ are ridden by more than a million people each day.

2. Subway commuters riding back and forth on the subways daily become accustomed to many inconveniences.

3. Standing room only which is a major inconvenience occurs regularly during rush hours.

4. Pushing and shoving to board the train is an everyday happening.

5. Dank stations whose walls drip dirty water are common sights.

6. Blaring stereos which are played at brain-piercing volumes provide background traveling music.

7. Some unhappy commuters who are trying to make using the subway system more pleasant have convinced officials to put poems where there would normally be advertising.

8. Buses which are the alternative to subways lack some of the negatives associated with train travel.

9. Bus riders who don't seem to be as aggressive as train riders may be more mellow than train passengers because bus travel is less stressful.

Extend: Write three to five sentences about public transportation that contain an unnecessary phrase or clause (nonrestrictive). Make sure to set off the nonessential material with commas.

© Houghton Mifflin Harcourt Publishing Company

TEKS 9.17A(ii), 9.18B(ii)

Commas with Nonrestrictive Phrases and Clauses 3

Commas are used to set off nonrestrictive phrases and clauses from the rest of a sentence. Nonrestrictive phrases and clauses can be removed from a sentence without changing the basic meaning. Turn to 666.2 in *Write Source* for more information.

> **Place commas around the nonrestrictive phrases and clauses in the sentences below.**

1. Nolan Ryan, who could throw a fastball close to 100 mph, says many of his 5,714 strikeouts came on the curveball.

2. Ryan's coach said, "The hitter would see the curveball that was coming at his head and freeze."

3. The curveball which is also called the "hook," the "snapdragon," or "Uncle Charlie" has long been a part of American baseball.

4. Little League pitchers who dream about throwing their first curveball may never get the chance.

5. The curveball that famous all-American pitch has helped pitchers become heroes, but the curveball is going out of style.

6. The curveball is being replaced by other breaking pitches which have names like "slider," "sinker," "split-finger fastball," and "knuckleball."

7. Today most pitching staffs in the major leagues have only one pitcher who throws a curveball.

8. The slider which is easier to learn and easier to control has become the preferred breaking pitch.

9. Pitchers who learn to throw a slider lose their ability to throw a curveball because each pitch uses a different set of muscles.

10. Steve Stone who won 25 games and a Cy Young Award in 1980 admits he overused the curveball and never pitched as well again.

© Houghton Mifflin Harcourt Publishing Company

TEKS 9.17A(ii), 9.18B(ii)

11. When pitchers throw a curveball which sometimes starts high and drops low they must control both the direction and the distance.

12. If young people whose muscles and bones aren't fully developed throw breaking balls, they risk forming certain types of calcium deposits.

13. Young people who practice pitching should wait until they are older before throwing curveballs and other breaking balls.

14. The advice that comes from professional pitchers is to wait until age 15 or 16.

Write answers to the following questions.

1. Which words introduce the nonrestrictive and restrictive clauses in sentences 11–14 above? (List them.) _____

_____

2. What are these words called? Turn to 535.2 and the chart on page 535 in *Write Source*. _____

3. Why is this name a good choice? _____

_____

_____

_____

Extend: Explore the sentences in this exercise. (You may wish to work with a partner.) Find and underline with one line the nouns that the nonrestrictive and restrictive clauses modify. Then find the special pronouns at the beginning of each clause and underline them with two lines. Turn to page 747 for information about nouns and 750.1 and 752.2 in *Write Source* for information about relative pronouns.

© Houghton Mifflin Harcourt Publishing Company

Other Uses for Commas

Commas are used to set off contrasted elements, such as those preceded by *not* (turn to 662.3 in *Write Source*); to set off dates (668.1); to set off items in addresses (668.2); to show hundreds, thousands, millions, and so forth in numbers (668.3); to set off the exact words of a speaker (670.1); and to separate a noun of direct address from the rest of the sentence (670.4).

> **Place commas where they are needed in the following sentences.**

1   Oprah Winfrey said "Lots of people want to ride with you in the limo,

2   but what you want is someone who will take the bus with you when the

3   limo breaks down."

4   "I think" Bill said "that Oprah Winfrey made a wise statement."

5   "Yes" Sarah replied "and when I'm famous, you can ride in my limo."

6   "How are you going to become famous Sarah?" Bill asked.

7   "When I live at 1600 Pennsylvania Avenue NW Washington D.C.

8   20006, I'll be famous" Sarah said.

9   "So you plan to marry the president of the United States" said Bill.

10 "No" Sarah said "I plan to be the president of the United States not

11 the first lady. Or maybe I'll be a pilot and fly an SR-71 reconnaissance

12 plane for 3000 miles at an altitude of 80000 feet" Sarah replied.

13 Bill said "Maybe you can become famous by making people laugh."

14 "Good idea" Sarah replied. "I'll be a famous emcee on a game show.

15 How's this: Do you know which *state* not nation produces more than

16 784000 tons of alfalfa annually?"

17 "No Sarah and no normal person would" Bill answered.

18 "Well Bill if you want to be a contestant on my game show, you'll

19 have to know things like that."

Extend: Write a dialogue between yourself and someone you know about being famous. Use quotation marks and commas correctly. Exchange papers with a classmate and check each other's work.

© Houghton Mifflin Harcourt Publishing Company

20

TEKS 9.18B, 9.18B(ii)

Review: Commas 2

> **Place commas where they are needed in the sentences below.**

1 The story of Paricutin, a volcano formed recently in Mexico, is an
2 interesting one. On February 20 1943 a local farmer who had stopped to
3 rest while plowing was startled by a column of smoke rising from the
4 middle of his cornfield. Assuming that he must have somehow started a
5 fire he rushed to put it out. He thought the smoke was coming from an
6 open fire but he found that the smoke was coming from a small hole in
7 the ground. The farmer thought for a moment about how to put out this
8 underground fire and then he put a stone over the hole. He checked the
9 hole later and was alarmed by the increase of dense black smoke. The
10 farmer recalled feeling the ground tremble and he noted that the soil
11 felt hotter than ever under his bare feet. He hurried to town to tell the
12 mayor and to bring some people back with him.

13 When they arrived some time later they saw black smoke billowing
14 from a hole 30 feet deep. The first explosion came that very night when
15 a thick column of smoke cinders and ash shot upward for more than a
16 mile. Explosions followed every few seconds; rocks which varied in size
17 from that of a walnut to that of a house were hurled into the air. Lava
18 began to flow two days later and the volcano continued to erupt for many
19 months. The lava flows and ash showers obliterated surrounding farms
20 forests and villages. Paricutin the first town destroyed by the eruption
21 gave up its very name to the new "mountain of fire."

© Houghton Mifflin Harcourt Publishing Company

TEKS 9.18B

Semicolons to Join Independent Clauses

Semicolons can join independent clauses in two ways, as shown in the examples below. Look for more information at 672.1 and 672.2 in *Write Source*.

> **Humpback whales are the slowest moving of all whales; they are also the most playful.** (The semicolon connects two independent clauses.)

> **Humpback whales are very social whales; therefore, they take time to play.** (The semicolon is often used with a conjunctive adverb. Note where to place the semicolon and comma.)

Place semicolons where needed in the following sentences. Add commas where necessary.

1. Humpback whales migrate every year they spend the summers in cool northern waters.

2. These whales can't smell, taste, or see well however they have excellent hearing.

3. The calves drink up to two gallons of milk per feeding they may feed 48 times per day.

4. At this rate they gain up to 200 pounds a day moreover they grow nearly a foot a week.

5. Humpback whales are disappearing at an alarming rate their population has dwindled from 102,000 to 8,700.

6. Humpbacks lift their bodies almost completely out of the water this is called "breaching."

7. Humpbacks also point their heads down toward the ocean's floor and make sounds this is called "singing."

8. No one knows why whales sing perhaps it is one of the ways they communicate.

9. Many whale species "sing" still the best singers are the humpbacks.

10. Humpbacks are called "floaters" they float when they die.

© Houghton Mifflin Harcourt Publishing Company

11. Humpbacks breathe in through two nostrils called blowholes then they exhale a spout of water vapor.

12. Humpbacks hit the water with their huge flippers the sound can be heard for miles and miles.

13. Humpbacks breach and slap water therefore people love to watch them.

14. Adult humpbacks weigh about 40 tons however they can leap about 50 feet into the air.

Write sentences according to the directions listed below.

1. Join two clauses with a conjunctive adverb. Use a semicolon and a comma correctly.

_____

_____

2. Join two independent clauses. Use a semicolon.

_____

_____

3. Join two clauses with the conjunctive adverb _however_. Use a semicolon and a comma correctly.

_____

_____

4. Join two independent clauses using a semicolon correctly.

_____

_____

5. Join two clauses with the conjunctive adverb _instead_. Use a semicolon and a comma correctly.

_____

_____

© Houghton Mifflin Harcourt Publishing Company

Hyphens 1

Use hyphens in the following situations: to form compound words, to join a capital letter to a noun or participle, to write out numbers from twenty-one to ninety-nine, and to join two or more words that serve as a single adjective.

> **My great-grandmother wrote a diary.**
> (*Great-grandmother* is a compound word. Turn to 676.1.)

> **She never wore a T-shirt!**
> (*T-shirt* is a word made by joining a capital letter to a noun. Turn to 676.4.)

> **She was twenty-two when she came to America.**
> (*Twenty-two* is a compound number. Turn to 678.1.)

> **She and Grandpa, both Swedish-speaking immigrants, opened a bakery.**
> (*Swedish-speaking* serves as a single adjective. Turn to 676.3.)

Insert hyphens where needed in the following sentences.

1. I was a smart six-year-old when I first met my great-grandmother.

2. I remember it was a not so pleasant day, even though she had made some delicious orange juice.

3. My forty two year old father had lost his job the day before.

4. He was working in a fast growing business.

5. He said, "I don't have state of the art computer skills, and I need them."

6. My great grandmother said, "You can make a U turn in your career and go back and learn them."

7. "I'm too old. I'm an over the hill student," he said.

8. My great grandmother laughed and said, "Yesterday I replaced my out of date printer with a new laserjet model."

9. My great uncles and great aunts laughed.

10. My father smiled and said, "Well, maybe forty two isn't over the hill."

Extend: Write four sentences about one or two of your relatives. In each sentence, include a different type of hyphenated word as explained in the previous exercise.

© Houghton Mifflin Harcourt Publishing Company

TEKS 9.18B

Hyphens 2

A hyphen is often used to make new words beginning with the prefixes *self-, ex-, all-, great-,* and *half-*. A hyphen is used to join numbers indicating the life span of a person and the score in a contest or vote. A hyphen is also used to separate a word at the end of a line of print.

> **Self-respect is necessary before you can respect others.**
> (A hyphen is usually used to form a word with the prefix *self-*. Turn to 676.2.)

> **Eleanor Roosevelt (1884–1962) was a writer and U.N. delegate.**
> (A hyphen is used to join numbers indicating a life span. Turn to 678.3.)

> **The city council voted 34–8 for a new public library.**
> (A hyphen is used to join numbers in a vote or a game score. Turn to 678.3.)

Use hyphens to show where the following words can be divided at the end of a line. Note that some should *not* be divided. Refer to 678.5 in *Write Source* and use a dictionary.

1. winning _____win-ning_____   6. brother-in-law _____
2. sometimes _____   7. loosen _____
3. wouldn't _____   8. delicate _____
4. central _____   9. equal _____
5. drama _____   10. among _____

Place hyphens where needed in the following sentences.

1. Franklin Delano Roosevelt (1882 1945) was our thirty-second president.

2. During his presidential terms (1933 1945), World War II began.

3. In Roosevelt's first election, he was elected by an electoral vote of 472 59.

4. Who was president during the post depression years?

5. Franklin Delano Roosevelt was an ex governor of which state?

6. His cousin Theodore Roosevelt (1858 1919) was the twenty-sixth president.

7. Congress voted unanimously 82 0 to enter World War II.

8. The support was anything but half hearted.

© Houghton Mifflin Harcourt Publishing Company

TEKS 9.18B(iii)
ELPS 5G

Dashes

Dashes are commonly used to emphasize parenthetical material—material that explains or clarifies but could be omitted. Turn to 692.1–692.5 in *Write Source* for other ways that dashes are used. Read the explanations and study the examples.

> **Insert** dashes where they can be used in the following sentences.

1. Ernest Shackleton had one goal and one goal only to travel all the way across Antarctica.

2. Shackleton's ship, *Endurance* an appropriate name as it turned out was caught in heavy ice and crushed in October 1915.

3. Shackleton and his crew endured eating penguin and seal blubber five long months adrift on an ice floe.

4. Eventually they found Elephant Island a tiny, windswept place hundreds of miles from civilization.

5. Ernest Shackleton amazed the world in fact, stunned the world when he and his entire crew survived.

6. "You aren't you can't be Ernest Shackleton," said the man at the whaling station on the island of South Georgia when Shackleton arrived.

7. "I am Ernest Shackleton. You thought me doomed? You thought me and my men" He could say no more.

8. Not one member of the crew died not in the entire 22-month ordeal of cold, hunger, and danger.

9. Six years later, in 1922, Shackleton died of a heart attack on South Georgia Island en route to where else? Antarctica.

Extend: Imagine you are Shackleton or one of his crew. Write about your ordeal. Use dashes in as many ways as you can—enclose a sudden break, show faltering speech, emphasize a word or phrase or clause, show missing words or letters, or set off an introductory series.

© Houghton Mifflin Harcourt Publishing Company

TEKS 9.18B, 9.18B(iii)

Review: Hyphens & Dashes

Place hyphens where needed in the following words and phrases.

1. great-great-grandfather
2. cheese filled celery sticks
3. four tenths
4. four, six, and eight inch widths
5. score of 11 9
6. ex mayor
7. big boned athlete
8. twelve year old boy
9. great aunt
10. all conference team
11. six year old girl
12. U turn
13. 1908 2000 C.E.
14. T shirt
15. vote of 321 642
16. mid May
17. state of the art technology
18. self respect
19. nine tenths
20. all out effort

Place dashes in the following sentences.

1. In 1941, when the United States entered World War II, the U.S. Army Air Corps-later the United States Air Force-needed pilots desperately.
2. Chuck Yeager only 19 years old joined the corps.
3. His talent for flying seemed to be a natural gift a gift that made him an incredible pilot and true ace.
4. Then, on his ninth mission, tragedy struck the American ace was shot down.
5. He parachuted to the ground wounded, bleeding, no feeling in his legs somewhere in German-occupied France.
6. Incredibly, he escaped all the way across the Pyrenees Mountains into Spain he even helped the French Underground along the way!

© Houghton Mifflin Harcourt Publishing Company

TEKS 9.18B
ELPS 5E

Apostrophes in Contractions & to Show Omitted Letters or Numbers

An apostrophe is used to make a contraction *(can't)*. An apostrophe is also used to show that letters have been omitted in words or numbers that are spelled as they are actually spoken *(good mornin'* and *class of '99)*. Turn to 680.1 in *Write Source*.

> **Place** apostrophes where needed in the following sentences.

1. "Dont you like asparagus?" Mom asked.

2. "I cant eat that green stuff," my little brother grumbled.

3. "Well, then Ill serve you purple vegetables," said Mom.

4. "You cant find any purple vegetables," said my little brother.

5. "Isnt eggplant purple?" my mother said to me.

6. "Im not sure. Maybe it is, but he wont eat it," I responded.

7. "No, I suppose youre right," Mom sighed.

8. She added, "Ive tried everything to get him to eat vegetables."

9. "Ill see if I can influence him," said Dad.

10. "If you eat your vegetables, Ill take you for a ride in the 57 Chevy convertible," said Dad.

11. Dad had restored this classic car during the summer of 09.

12. It wasnt his first car, but it was his favorite.

13. Hed always driven it in the homecoming parade with a banner that said "Class of 85" on it.

14. "I sure dont like vegetables, but I sure like ridin in that car," said my little brother.

15. "Well then, well go right after you eat your vegetables," said Dad.

Extend: Write a conversation between yourself and a cousin (or friend) about something you did together when you were little. Include some contractions in the conversation, and challenge yourself by including some numbers and words that need apostrophes because they are spelled as they are actually spoken.

© Houghton Mifflin Harcourt Publishing Company

TEKS 9.18B
ELPS 5E

Apostrophes to Form Possessives 1

Use apostrophes to show possession. Turn to 680.2–682.2 in *Write Source*.

> **Grandpa's hair, Chicago's wind, men's room, woman's office**
> (When a word—either singular or plural—does not end in *s*, add an apostrophe and *s* to form the possessive.)

> **players' uniforms, lawyers' arguments, dogs' collars**
> (When the plural of a word ends in *s*, add only an apostrophe.)

> **great-grandma's diary, somebody's house, son-in-law's job**
> (In compound words, make only the last word possessive.)

Place apostrophes in each of the following phrases to show possession.

1. Jane's prom dress 2. the towns climate 3. mens clothes 4. daughter-in-laws teeth (singular) 5. the womens exercises 6. that girls opinions 7. all the girls clothes (plural) 8. childrens rooms 9. loves blessings 10. someones beauty 11. the cows path (plural) 12. babys crib 13. babies rattles 14. a months work 15. the journeys itinerary 16. stairs carpeting (plural) 17. a years passage 18. a headlights beam 19. the headlights beams 20. peoples judgments

Write sentences containing possessives using the instructions below.

1. Show that one boy owns two dogs, and both dogs need a bath.
   Jack's dogs, Sam and Beauty, need a bath.

2. Show that both of your great-grandmothers kept diaries.
   _____

3. Show that a hat, a pair of shoes, and a coat left on the porch belong to John.
   _____

4. Show that apples and chicken are favorite foods for both Ceema and Anna.
   _____

Extend: Write instructions for three sentences that contain possessives (as in the exercise above). Exchange instructions with a classmate and complete each other's exercise.

© Houghton Mifflin Harcourt Publishing Company

TEKS 9.18B
ELPS 5E

Apostrophes to Form Possessives 2

> **Brown, Jenkins, and Smith's law firm**
> (When possession is shared by more than one noun, use the possessive form for the last noun in the series. Turn to 680.4.)

> **Brown's, Jenkins', and Smith's law firms**
> (When possession is individual, make each noun possessive. Turn to 680.2.)

> **boss's salary, Kiss's album** (When a singular noun ends in *s*, there are two ways to form the possessive. If the word has one syllable and can be pronounced easily, add an apostrophe and *s*. Turn to 680.3.)

> **Ramses' tomb** (The other way is to add only an apostrophe. This is recommended when adding an *s* to the word would make the pronunciation difficult—*Moses's staff* or *Sophocles's plays*. Adding only an apostrophe is preferred for words of more than one syllable. Turn to 680.3.)

Place an apostrophe and *s* where needed to form possessives in the following phrases.

1. Dad and Mom ᵛ⁄s horse **2.** Molly, Polly, and Mom vacation **3.** George and Sam

lunches **4.** the lion and the horse manes **5.** our town and their town festivals

6. Jane and Sal dog **7.** the car and the truck headlights **8.** the boy and the girl

chairs **9.** Moss elephants **10.** Adam and Lois address

Write the plural, as well as the singular and plural possessives, for the words below.

	Plural	Possessive Singular	Possessive Plural
1. child	*children*	*child's*	*children's*
2. man			
3. mother-in-law			
4. lady			
5. woman			

Extend: Write sentences for the five words listed above. Practice forming both singular and plural possessives.

© Houghton Mifflin Harcourt Publishing Company

TEKS 9.18B
ELPS 5E

Review: Apostrophes

> **Write** the possessive form or the contraction for the underlined word or words.

Tena/Dorothy's   **1.** Tena and Dorothy grandfather is 82 years old.

_____ **2.** Dean and Marvin sleeping bags got wet in the rain.

_____ **3.** The commander in chief desk was always neat.

_____ **4.** The basketball players uniforms were scattered over the floor. (_Players_ is plural.)

_____ **5.** Havent you finished the test?

_____ **6.** My sister-in-law hobby is swimming.

_____ **7.** The children band is playing at 7 P.M.

_____ **8.** The cities mayors all met in Washington.

_____ **9.** Isnt there a better answer to the problem?

_____ **10.** Felipe textbooks are lying in the cafeteria.

_____ **11.** The principal disciplinary actions were fair.

_____ **12.** Both of the girls baseball uniforms are hanging up in the bus. (One girl owns both uniforms.)

_____ **13.** Harlen, Charlie, and Ron raft floated away.

_____ **14.** Laura, Linda, and Latonya fathers will help them.

_____ **15.** The class future is uncertain.

_____ **16.** The coach whistle was plugged.

_____ **17.** The mens meeting is finished.

_____ **18.** He mumbled, "I cant remember."

_____ **19.** Why dont you write some more sentences?

_____ **20.** I cant think of anything more to write.

© Houghton Mifflin Harcourt Publishing Company

 **TEKS** 9.18B, 9.18B(i)

Quotation Marks with Titles & Special Words

Quotation marks are used to punctuate titles of songs, short poems, short stories, lectures, episodes from radio and television programs, chapters of books, unpublished works, and articles from newspapers, magazines, and encyclopedias. Quotation marks are also used to point out a word that is being used in a special way, such as ironically or sarcastically (not in a genuine or sincere sense), or to indicate that a word is slang. Turn to 686.2–686.3 in *Write Source*.

> **I heard Samuel Barber's "Knoxville: Summer of 1915" last night.**
> (Use quotation marks around the name of a song.)

> **I was amazed that a "boring" old song could be so moving.**
> (Quotation marks point out a word being used ironically.)

> **It's a "cool" piece of music about a hot summer night.**
> (Quotation marks indicate that a word is slang.)

Write sentences below using quotation marks correctly.

1. Include the title of your favorite song in a sentence.

   "Row, Row, Row Your Boat" is my favorite camp song.

2. Use a short story title in a sentence.

   _____

3. Use a word or phrase ironically or sarcastically in a sentence.

   _____

4. Use one of your favorite slang words in a sentence.

   _____

5. Make up the title of a magazine article and use it in a sentence.

   _____

6. Write a sentence using one of these words—*guide, green, honesty*—in a special way.

   _____

   _____

Extend: List five titles that would require quotation marks. Ask a classmate to write sentences using the titles and to use quotation marks correctly. Check each other's work.

© Houghton Mifflin Harcourt Publishing Company

TEKS 9.18B
ELPS 5G

Quotation Marks with Dialogue

Use quotation marks to punctuate dialogue. Study the examples below to see where other punctuation marks are placed. Turn to 684.1, 684.2, and 686.1 in *Write Source*.

> **"Today we are going down into the Grand Canyon," said Mr. Thomas. "It will be a grand journey."** (A period follows *Thomas* because the preceding quotation is a complete sentence. Notice where the quotation marks are placed.)

> **"Well," said Jane, "that's impossible!"**
> (A comma follows *Jane* because what follows completes the sentence.)

> **"How can we go down into the Grand Canyon while sitting in our desks?" Tony asked.** (The question mark is placed inside the quotation marks because the quotation is a question.)

Punctuate the following sentences with quotation marks, commas, and end marks.

1. "We will pretend," said Mr. Thomas. "When I put a slide on the screen, you ask questions and make comments as if you are really there."

2. I recognize that place whispered Colleen

3. What river is that asked Mark

4. I know said Jack It's the Colorado River. It has carved its way down through all that rock making the Grand Canyon

5. I don't believe it said Miesha How long has it been carving the rocks

6. Well, you'll find this hard to believe, too, Miesha, but the Colorado River has been carving the Grand Canyon for about 6 million years replied Mr. Thomas.

7. How wide is the canyon? asked Roger

8. Mr. Thomas replied It's at least 10 miles across

9. How deep is the Grand Canyon asked Roger I'm getting dizzy up here

10. I know It's a mile deep laughed Jane

Extend: Imagine you are visiting a famous place with your friends or family. Write a dialogue about it, punctuating it carefully. If you choose a place you have actually seen, it will be easier to include interesting descriptive details. Otherwise, use an encyclopedia to learn more about a place you would like to visit someday.

© Houghton Mifflin Harcourt Publishing Company

TEKS 9.18B

Quotation Marks & Diagonals

> **Place** quotation marks where needed in the following student essay, "Poets Are Different." When placing diagonals (slash marks) in the poem, which is included in the essay, remember that each new line of poetry begins with a capital letter. Turn to 684.1–686.2 and 690.4 in *Write Source*.

1   One of my teachers said, "All I can say is that poets are different from

2   the people I live with and different from me. And, yet, I honor them in

3   some way . . . some way that I can't quite label." That's how I feel, too.

4   Sometimes my mind says *yes* when I read a poet's words. This

5   happens when I read these lines by Thoreau: A lake is the landscape's

6   most beautiful and expressive feature. It is earth's eye . . . .

7   Sometimes my mind says *no!* For instance, whenever I read this line

8   by Walt Whitman, the "no" happens: the delicious singing of the mother.

9   How can singing be delicious? Grilled steak and a baked potato (loaded)

10 are delicious.

11   Have you ever read Victory in the Eye of the Beholder? It's about a

12 baseball game. The poet writes the lines like this:

13   Their hero swings And the ball rockets away. Fielders run Calling,

14   "I've got it, I've got it!" But the fans know better And the ball sails

15   on. Like a giant wave, They stand to their feet once more Yelling his

16   name As he stomps on homeplate And bows deeply to the crowd. The

17   game is theirs.

Extend: Create three to five sentences about song lyrics that demonstrate the rules for using quotation marks. Turn to 684.1–686.2 in *Write Source*.

© Houghton Mifflin Harcourt Publishing Company

Italics (Underlining) & Quotation Marks

Italics is a printer's term for a style of type that is slightly slanted. In material that is handwritten or typed on a machine that cannot print in italics, each word or letter that should be in italics is underlined.

Italics (underlining) is used to indicate the titles of magazines, newspapers, pamphlets, books, plays, films, radio and television programs, book-length poems, ballets, operas, lengthy musical compositions, albums (such as CD's), legal cases, the names of ships and aircraft, scientific names, and foreign words. Turn to 688.1–688.4 in *Write Source*.

Quotation marks are also used to indicate some titles. Turn to 686.3 and 688.1–688.2 in *Write Source* to help you decide when to use quotation marks and when to underline or use italics.

> **Write** a **Q** in the blank if quotation marks should be used or a **U** if underlining should be used.

_U_ 1. Titanic *(ship)*

2. America the Beautiful *(song)*

3. an opera

4. Reader's Digest *(magazine)*

5. radio program

6. Jurassic Park *(novel)*

7. magazine article

8. television episode

9. television program

10. Brown vs. Brown *(legal case)*

11. bonjour *(French)*

12. To Kill a Mockingbird *(book)*

13. Los Angeles Times *(newspaper)*

14. short story

15. radio episode

16. The Raven *(poem)*

17. yucca brevifolia *(Joshua tree)*

18. pamphlet

19. Jack and Jill *(nursery rhyme)*

20. Macbeth *(play)*

21. movie

22. CD

23. chapter in a book

24. speech or lecture title

Extend: Write a paragraph that includes the titles of your favorite movie, TV show, song, album, magazine, novel, and short story. Try to include at least seven titles. Use quotation marks and italics (underlining) correctly.

© Houghton Mifflin Harcourt Publishing Company

9.18B

Review: Quotation Marks & Italics (Underlining)

> **Add** quotation marks where they are needed. Underline words that should be in italics.

1. "Please pass the toast," she said.

2. The Conqueror Worm is a poem written by Edgar Allan Poe.

3. A Literary History of the United States is a fine resource book.

4. Why did you play my Rock 'n' Roll Racing? Justin asked.

5. I had to, said Benji, because mine was broken.

6. He likes clunky because the word is onomatopoeic.

7. Formal writing does not use phrases like that's really awesome or far out.

8. Gone with the Wind is an exciting film that is still respected today.

9. The Greek word Kalimera means the same as the German words guten tag.

10. The city paper Daily Tribune carried an article entitled Foot Lake Will Be Cleaned.

11. Did you study Faulkner's short story Two Soldiers? she asked.

12. No, he replied, we read Thurber's short story Catbird Seat last week.

13. Does your group sing America the Beautiful? she asked.

14. Aunt Midge calls Billy her Kleines Kind.

15. I'm glad I didn't sail on the Titanic.

16. The Great Gatsby is F. Scott Fitzgerald's most popular novel.

17. Dave Matthews has recorded many CD's, but Crash is probably his best.

18. That's fine, she said, but who wants to read his essay The Incredible Journey?

19. I do, Jordan replied.

© Houghton Mifflin Harcourt Publishing Company

★ TEKS 9.18B

Punctuation in Math

Look at the following examples of how to use punctuation in math.

> **There are more than 200 billion stars in the known universe—that's more than 200,000,000,000.** (The commas separate a series of numbers in order to distinguish hundreds, thousands, millions, and so on. Turn to 668.3.)

> **The sun, also a star, is only one-thousandth the diameter of the largest stars.** (The hyphen is used between elements of a fraction. Turn to 678.1.)

> **Astronomers measure the distance to stars in light-years. One light-year is 5.88 trillion miles.** (The period is used as a decimal point. Turn to 659.3.)

> **Other than the sun, the nearest star is 4.3 light-years (25 trillion miles) away.** (Parentheses are used to enclose supplementary information. See 690.1.)

> **Stars are 3/4 hydrogen and almost 1/4 helium.** (The diagonal forms a fraction.)

Insert the correct punctuation in the following sentences.

1. Red stars are about 5,000° F (2,800° C) but blue stars can be up to 50,000° F (28,000° C).

2. A yellowish star, like our sun, is only one fifth the temperature of a blue star.

3. Supergiants, the largest of the stars, have diameters that are more than 1000 times larger than the sun's diameter.

4. White dwarfs are only 1 100 the size of the sun.

5. Some white dwarfs are only 5200 miles 8700 kilometers in diameter.

6. Star clusters are groups of 10000 to 1000000 densely packed stars.

7. In some clusters, stars can be less than one hundredth of a light-year 5880000000 miles away from each other.

8. Absolute magnitude is a star's brightness if the star were 326 (32 and six-tenths) light-years from the earth.

Extend: Write several sentences about what you are studying in math, science, accounting, or some other course in which numbers are often used. Use as many math punctuation marks as you can.

© Houghton Mifflin Harcourt Publishing Company

TEKS 9.18B

Other Forms of Punctuation 1

> **Review** the following uses of punctuation. Then write another example that uses the punctuation correctly.

1. I had just come home from school and reached into the mailbox . . . but there was nothing there. (The ellipsis indicates a pause. Turn to 694.3.)

_____

_____

2. I went home at four o'clock (?) before going to practice. (The question mark shows uncertainty. Turn to 660.2.)

_____

_____

3. It must have been my little brother (who else could it be?) who took my coat. (This question mark is used for a short question within parentheses. See 660.3.)

_____

_____

4. Cal Ripken, Jr., is one of the best baseball players ever. (Commas enclose the title "Jr." following the surname. See 668.4.)

_____

_____

5. Yeah, I think there's room for another person to come to the concert. (This comma sets off an interjection. Turn to 670.2.)

_____

_____

Extend: Write a conversation between yourself and a friend about going to a party. Try to use as many of the different punctuation marks in this exercise as you can.

© Houghton Mifflin Harcourt Publishing Company

TEKS 9.18B

Other Forms of Punctuation 2

> **Review** the following examples of punctuation. Then write another example that uses the punctuation correctly.

1. Mr. Smith, I need another day to finish the assignment because my computer crashed last night. (The comma separates the noun of address, *Mr. Smith.* See 670.4.)

_____

_____

2. We call him Dr. Hendrick because he has a Ph.D. in English literature (*Dr.* and *Ph.D.* require periods because they are abbreviations. See 668.4.)

_____

_____

3. Would you please hand me the five-, seven-, and nine-sixteenths sockets. (The hyphen is used in a series of two or more words that have a common element that is omitted until the last term. See 678.2.)

_____

_____

4. I opened the door slowly and saw who it was waiting in my room—my best friend, Jaime. (The dash is used to emphasize *my best friend, Jaime.* Turn to 692.5.)

_____

_____

5. Our basketball team is the crème de la crème. No one is going to beat us this year. (The underlining indicates a phrase of foreign words. See 688.4.)

_____

_____

Extend: Write five sentences requiring each of the types of punctuation above; however, don't punctuate your sentences. Exchange papers. Check each other's work.

© Houghton Mifflin Harcourt Publishing Company

TEKS 9.18A

Pretest: Capitalization

Cross out incorrect capitalization. If the word should be capitalized, write the letter above it. If the word should not be capitalized, do not write anything.

1. When the winds come rolling in over the ~~b~~lack ~~r~~ock ~~d~~esert near ~~r~~eno, ~~n~~evada,
   land "sailors" jump on their three-wheeled "boats" and catch a wild ride.
   (B R D R N written above)

2. Until recently, black rock's playa, or salt flats, was a place where few have
   visited. It's been called the "vacant heart of the west."

3. back in the 1800s, mormons and other Religious Groups crossed this dangerous
   wasteland looking for a place to worship god.

4. in 1849, they were followed by the forty-niners—the gold seekers, not the san
   francisco Football Team.

5. Shortly after the california gold rush, the western Pacific railroad built a track
   across the playa, making it easier for others to follow.

6. It was mainly chinese, irish, and african american labor that built the railroad.

7. However, when the laborers did not put down roots in the area, their mandarin,
   gaelic, and swahili languages disappeared.

8. Several Decades went by before someone discovered that the Desert was a
   perfect training ground for World war II aviators.

9. Because of its remote location and vast, flat expanses, the playa was chosen as
   the site of the first Supersonic Land speed record.

10. On wednesday, october 15, 1997, andy green and his british jet-propelled car,
    the *thrust ssc,* broke the Sound Barrier.

11. light fixtures were knocked off the ceilings in the town of gerlach, five miles
    away.

© Houghton Mifflin Harcourt Publishing Company

TEKS 9.18A

12. Rocket clubs, such as aero-pac, like the wide-open spaces to launch their hand-built rockets.

13. The faa (federal aviation administration) granted the clubs launch clearance to 100,000 feet.

14. The utah rocket club launches rockets in this desert.

15. The cost of launching rockets is shared by the Club.

16. The local justice of the peace, phil thomas, said festivals and speed records do not reflect the true rural nevada.

17. The desert there is an environment where hardworking people call their chevy, ford, or dodge pickups "aunt Betsy" or "father mulligan."

18. It is a place where democrats and republicans gather on dusty Street corners to argue Politics alongside Environmentalists and Farmers.

19. With all the recent activity, the u.s. bureau of land management has been working hard to manage the fragile ecology of the playa area.

© Houghton Mifflin Harcourt Publishing Company

Capitalization 1

One of the keys to correct capitalization is remembering to capitalize all proper nouns and proper adjectives. Review 698.1 in *Write Source*.

> **Cross out** incorrect capitalization and write the correct letter above it.

1. the legendary track star jesse owens was born on september 12, 1913, in the
   rural town of oakville, alabama.

   (handwritten corrections: T above "the", J above "jesse", O above "owens", S above "september", O above "oakville", A above "alabama")

2. boils, fevers, chest colds, and pneumonia plagued his childhood, but with hard

   work and help from friends like coach riley, jesse blossomed.

3. the owens family was poor; jesse's father was a sharecropper and his granddad

   was a former slave.

4. meat was served only on special occasions or holidays like christmas and easter.

5. jesse's parents held a powerful belief in god. as devout baptists, they helped

   their children memorize a different bible verse each sunday.

6. in 1922, the entire family, including aunt addie, moved to the north so that

   jesse's father, henry, could get a job in the steel mills.

7. jesse's mother, emma, thought that living north of the mason-dixon line would

   help the children get a better education.

8. in the south, jim crow laws created separate schools that segregated african

   american children from white children.

9. on his first day at bolton elementary school in ohio, james cleveland owens

   received the nickname that stuck with him for the rest of his life.

10. a teacher thought the young boy said his name was "jesse" when he had, in fact,

    shyly answered "j.c."

Extend: Write three to five sentences about a famous athlete, but don't capitalize the proper nouns or proper adjectives. Exchange your paper with a classmate and correct each other's capitalization.

© Houghton Mifflin Harcourt Publishing Company

 9.18A

Capitalization 2

Continue to explore specific uses of capitalization. Turn to *Write Source* 698.1–702.5.

> **Cross out** incorrect capitalization and write the correct letter above it.

1. $\overset{J}{\cancel{j}}$esse $\overset{O}{\cancel{o}}$wens always struggled with school, especially with $\overset{E}{\cancel{e}}$nglish and social studies, because of his illnesses and lack of early education.

2. jesse's winning personality and friendly nature helped him become student council president and captain of the basketball team at fairmount junior high.

3. in college, jesse owens was called the "buckeye bullet" from ohio state university.

4. it took only 45 minutes for jesse to smash three world records and tie a fourth during a track and field meet in ann arbor, michigan.

5. in 1936, jesse and the u.s. olympic track team sailed to europe from new york on a luxury steamship, the *s.s. manhattan*.

6. jesse won four gold medals in the olympic games in berlin, germany.

7. america was in the midst of the great depression, and americans were looking for a hero.

8. they found one in the national collegiate athletic association (ncaa) track star, jesse owens.

9. later he received the congressional medal of freedom for his work with underprivileged youth.

10. jesse owens is remembered today for his olympic medals, his ncaa records, and his dedication to youth.

Extend: Write five sentences that illustrate capitalization rules 700.2 through 700.6 in *Write Source*.

© Houghton Mifflin Harcourt Publishing Company

9.18A

Capitalization 3

Explore specific uses of capitalization. Turn to 698.1–702.5 in *Write Source*.

> **Cross out** incorrect capitalization and write the correct letter above it.

1. The great artist ~~n~~orman ~~r~~ockwell was born in ~~n~~ew ~~y~~ork ~~c~~ity in 1894.
   (corrections above: N R N Y C)

2. at age 15, rockwell enrolled at the national academy school.

3. later that year, he was asked to design his first works of art—christmas cards.

4. By the age of 20, rockwell had become art editor for *boys' life* magazine.

5. During world war I, rockwell was stationed in charleston, south carolina, but he continued to draw.

6. Much of his art dealt with his ideal of american patriotism and his love of small town america.

7. One of his pictures, called "a family tree," appeared on the cover of *the saturday evening post* in october 1959.

8. It humorously traces the ancestors of the "typical" u.s. family.

9. The picture shows how most americans represent not one but many nationalities and religions.

10. The limbs on the tree branch backward from the 1950s through the roaring twenties.

11. Ironically, the 1920s flapper has a protestant minister for a father.

12. The branches continue downward through the wild west of the late 1800s.

13. A cowboy's parents are a grizzled prospector and a beautiful navajo princess.

14. The grandparents are yankee and confederate soldiers, split during the civil war.

Extend: Write five sentences that illustrate capitalization rules 702.1 through 702.5 in *Write Source*.

© Houghton Mifflin Harcourt Publishing Company

46

Review: Capitalization

> **Cross out** incorrect capitalization and write the correct letter above it.

1.   *I*   *S* *A*
In the movie ̶sister ̶act 2, whoopi goldberg plays deloris, a las vegas lounge singer.

2. she is brought to the west coast by friends who are nuns.

3. deloris is asked to once again become sister mary clarence, the school's music teacher, and help keep their catholic school open.

4. if the school closes, the racially mixed neighborhood of latino, african american, and anglo residents will be without a school.

5. the sisters are upset because there will never be another christmas pageant, may crowning, or june graduation at st. francis high school.

6. the film's bad guy is the principal, mr. crisp, who wants to take an early retirement.

7. father wolfgang is the school chef whose "wurst" meal is his best. (he can cook only german sausage.)

8. the latin teacher, father thomas, is concerned; the mathematics teacher, father ignatius, is hopeful. or is it the other way around?

9. sister mary clarence knows the value of the old saying: "god helps those who help themselves."

10. sister mary clarence and her newly inspired students win a contest by performing a combination of gospel and rap music while using american sign language. (in the process, they save the school.)

© Houghton Mifflin Harcourt Publishing Company

Pretest: Numbers & Abbreviations

> **Write** the correct form (numerals, words, or letters) above the underlined numbers and abbreviations below. If the form is correct, write **C** above it.

1. _Two_ <u>2</u> of the _C_ <u>seven</u> contestants won a ribbon.

2. All <u>one thousand seventy nine</u> of the students took the ACT test today.

3. The population of that little village is <u>two hundred and fifty</u>.

4. The average temperature is <u>ninety</u> °F.

5. Did you put in <u>three</u> tbsp. of butter?

6. He was elected by a vote of <u>twenty-three to four</u>.

7. Remember your appointment is at <u>4:00 p.m</u>.

8. Did you say my appointment was at <u>4</u> o'clock?

9. I am <u>five'</u> and <u>seven"</u> tall.

10. He kept <u>8 percent</u> of the funds for himself.

11. Did you order <u>10 12-foot</u> subs for the party?

12. He was driving <u>thirty-five mph</u> in a <u>25 miles per hour</u> zone.

> **Write** abbreviations for the following words.

1. California _CA_ or _Calif._

2. Washington _____ or _____

3. Street _____

4. quart _____

5. as soon as possible _____

6. liter _____

7. Incorporated _____

8. and so forth _____

9. apartment _____

10. teaspoon _____

11. gallon _____

12. gross national product _____

13. kilogram _____

14. public relations _____

© Houghton Mifflin Harcourt Publishing Company

Numbers

In most contemporary writing, numbers below 10 are *usually* spelled out. Review 708.1–708.4 in *Write Source* before you do this exercise.

> **Underline** the misused numbers and write the correct versions above them.

1. *One-half*
   <u>1/2</u> salsa and 1/2 fusion, Latin music draws from many different Hispanic and Caribbean cultures.

2. Latinos currently make up more than fourteen percent of the United States population, and that number will increase to 15% by the year twenty twenty.

3. With several million listeners, *La Mega* ninety-seven point nine, a New York radio station, is one of the most popular Hispanic stations in the United States.

4. Despite such a large local audience, the Hispanic stations reach only about five % of the radio listeners.

5. This means Latin pop groups often cross over into English. One of these groups, Santana, has been crossing over for forty years.

6. Ricky Martin has had a number-one Spanish hit in 22 countries, including the United States.

7. Singing with the pop group Menudo made Martin famous, but singing the World Cup soccer anthem, *La Copa de la Vida,* at the nineteen-ninety-nine Grammy Awards made him an international superstar.

8. Another crossover singer, Cuban-born Gloria Estefan, and her husband, Emilio, head a two hundred million dollar music empire.

9. The 2 Estefans have also been ranked on the *Forbes* list of the five hundred wealthiest entertainers.

Extend: Write three to five sentences using lots of numbers. Exchange your sentences with a classmate. After completing each other's worksheets, check your answers.

© Houghton Mifflin Harcourt Publishing Company

Abbreviations, Acronyms, & Initialisms

In formal writing, most abbreviations are spelled out. Turn to 710.1–712.3 in *Write Source*.

Write the full word(s) above each underlined abbreviation. Use your handbook.

1. The following statements are based on *information* info found in *The Guinness Book of World Records*.

2. According to a spokesperson for the FmHA, Charles Houghton of New Boston, NH, grew a record 1,337-lb. pumpkin.

3. The youngest person to ever enter college was Michael Kearney, who entered Santa Rosa Jr. College at the age of six yrs., seven mos.

4. The fastest land bird on record was an ostrich clocked at 72 mph.

5. Willie Jones of Atlanta, GA, survived heatstroke despite a body temperature of 115 degrees F.

6. The FCC estimates that Paul Harvey's news program was the top radio show in 1996.

7. According to the FDIC, the Bank of East Asia, Ltd., has assets of $144 million.

8. The longest sausage ever made was 36 mi. and 1,320 yds. long.

9. Tyson Gay of Clermont, FL, USA, is the 2010 American record holder in the 100-m. dash.

10. Valued at 14 trillion dollars, the GNP for the U.S. is the largest in the world.

Extend: Imagine that you and some friends are forming a new club. Come up with three or four acronyms (and what they mean, of course) for the name of your club.

© Houghton Mifflin Harcourt Publishing Company

Review: Numbers & Abbreviations

Underline the incorrect usage of numbers and abbreviations in the following sentences. Write the corrections above.

1. The Panama Canal, located in what is now the <u>Rep.</u> *Republic* of Panama, has been called the "8th wonder of the world."

2. Located at approximately 80 deg. W. lat. and 10 deg. N. long., it has cut more than 7,800 mi. off the journey from one side of N. America to the other.

3. The canal saves wks.—if not mths.—of travel around Cape Horn.

4. A railroad across Panama was built 1st in 1855, but that construction claimed the lives of more than six thousand workers, mostly from disease.

5. After France failed to complete the Pan. Canal in 1904, Pres. Teddy Roosevelt proposed that the U.S. take over the project.

6. Before the canal could be built, the worker pop. had to be protected from yellow fever, malaria, and smallpox.

7. Col. Wm. Gorgas solved the problem with gals. of kerosene, lbs. of soap, and tons of pyrethrum powder.

8. On Aug. 15, 1914, a cement boat called the *Ancon* was the 1st ship to use the Panama Canal.

9. The canal's locks are 110 ft. wide by 1,000 ft. long by 23 yds. deep.

10. The total cost was $380,000,000, which would be more than the entire La. Purchase.

11. The canal is still used today, 97 yrs. after opening.

12. Cargo ships cut 100's of hrs. from their sailing time by using the Pan. Canal.

© Houghton Mifflin Harcourt Publishing Company

TEKS 9.19
ELPS 5C

Pretest: Plurals & Spelling

> **Write the correct plural form above all the underlined words.**

1. The canyon echoed with the thunder from the <u>hoof</u> of the stampeding mustangs.

2. Most of my <u>hunch</u> turn out to be correct.

3. Both <u>bakery</u> had many <u>loaf</u> of bread on display.

4. <u>Pizza</u> in Italy are often made with sun-dried <u>tomato</u>.

5. The <u>radius</u> of the circles were equal.

6. The stray dog ate three <u>bowlful</u> of food.

7. How many <u>wife</u> did King Henry VIII have altogether?

8. The <u>alto</u> needed to sing louder, or they would not have been heard above the <u>soprano</u>.

9. Both disc <u>jockey</u> had huge collections of <u>CD</u>.

> **Write the correct spelling above each misspelled word in the following sentences.**

1. A driver's lisence lists the person's hieght and waight.

2. The preliminery vote in Britain's Parlament was in favor of the Labour Party.

3. The writting under the photograph was almost illegable.

4. It is quiet likeley that the liutenent told the sargent to ship the missales.

5. The libary has the origenal copy of the manuscrip.

6. There was not enough spaggetti to feed the majorety of the students.

7. Insidently, I hope you have desided to enter the compitition.

8. It is probebly uneccesary to write the messege in more than two parragraphs.

9. The atheletes left their street close in the gymnaseum's locker room.

10. Her incredeble courage was accknowleged and apreciated.

© Houghton Mifflin Harcourt Publishing Company

TEKS 9.19
ELPS 5C

Plurals 1

Learning the rules for forming plurals helps you become a good speller. Turn to 704.1–706.4 in *Write Source*.

> **Write** the correct plural form above each underlined noun. Put a *C* above any underlined word that is correct.

1. My relatives are Montana <u>cowboy</u> [*cowboys*] who work the <u>ranch</u> [*ranches*] where the deer and the <u>antelope</u> [*C*] play.

2. Uncle Clem uses <u>bagful</u> of colorful western slang.

3. He brags that his boots are so fine, you can see the <u>callus</u> on his <u>toes</u>.

4. And he insists that his <u>sneeze</u> are louder than two <u>bullfrog</u> with a bullhorn.

5. Aunt Maggie says he couldn't carry a tune even if the <u>banjo</u> had two <u>handle</u>.

6. When he sings "<u>Penny</u> from Heaven," it sounds more like howling.

7. Clem likes to say that his <u>brother-in-law</u>, Jake and Randy, are as quiet as <u>sheep</u> with their <u>mouth</u> full.

8. He says it was once so hot, the <u>cactus</u> melted.

9. One time, when I asked why bandits wore <u>handkerchief</u> over their noses, he replied, "Because bandits don't take baths, that's why."

10. Uncle Clem claims his favorite meal is <u>potato</u> and <u>quail</u>.

11. He has been known to eat five <u>plateful</u> of <u>potato</u> and two <u>loaf</u> of bread at a single meal.

12. Once, when I used one of his best <u>knife</u> to whittle, I could hear him screeching louder than three <u>coyote</u> in a gunnysack.

Extend: Write four to six sentences about a one-of-a-kind person you know. Include at least one plural in each sentence, and check your spelling.

© Houghton Mifflin Harcourt Publishing Company

Plurals 2

Here are more plurals for you to practice with. Review 704.1–706.4 in *Write Source*.

> **Write** the correct plural form above each underlined word.

1. Last summer I visited St. Petersburg, one of the great, ancient *cities* city of Russia.

2. The day I remember best was when I went to the city park and watched as men of all <u>age</u> swapped <u>story</u> and played board games.

3. I was surprised that I did not see any <u>female</u>, so I asked why there were no <u>woman</u> present.

4. They replied that their <u>wife</u> were not invited to join them, even if the women were smart and had <u>Ph.D.</u>

5. The men assumed the women socialized while shopping at the fruit, vegetable, and meat <u>market</u>.

6. <u>Eyebrow</u> went up when I asked them to teach me the <u>rule</u> for the game of *nardo,* but they graciously showed me how to play.

7. I saw that the games were played on oval-shaped <u>board</u> that were held together with <u>hinge</u>.

8. Like the American game of backgammon, *nardo* uses two <u>die</u>.

9. Whenever fives and <u>six</u> were rolled, the *nardo* players yelled, *"Shesh-besh!"*

10. Meanwhile, on another set of <u>bench</u>, four men were hunched over a game of <u>domino</u>.

11. All around us, <u>handful</u> of vendors sold <u>sausage</u> and hot tea.

12. A musician played soft mandolin <u>solo</u> elsewhere in the park.

13. I have many wonderful <u>memory</u> of my visit to Russia.

Extend: Write a short paragraph about a visit you made to a different place—near or far. Include plural words whenever possible, checking to make sure you've spelled them correctly.

© Houghton Mifflin Harcourt Publishing Company

TEKS 9.19
ELPS 5C

Spelling 1

Spelling can be tricky. You must learn the rules as well as the exceptions to the rules. Turn to pages 714–719 in *Write Source*.

> **Underline** the words that are misspelled and write the correct words above.

desperately

1. I <u>desparately</u> want to make the basketball team.

2. I think I have enough heigth and weigth.

3. My strenth and stamina are as good as any of the other kids' in my school.

4. I'm a good ahtlete.

5. Dribbling is more easly done than shooting free throws—at least for me.

6. If I don't make the team, the coach will ask me to be the "apprentise" again.

7. I'll run errands, get water, distribut towels, congratalate the team members, and

hide my misary.

8. My parents try to sheild me from possible disapointment.

9. Mom says, "It's possibel you won't make the team, but you can always try again."

10. Dad says, "Prehaps you'll make it this time."

11. My impatiense grows daily.

12. I think I'll join the drum and bugle core if I don't make the basketball team.

13. I'll have a briused ego, that's for sure—especially if my cousen makes the team and

I don't.

14. I think I'd like steping out onto the floor following my interduction.

15. Some of the teams we play in our division are feircely competetive.

16. It's finaly Wendesday, and guess what? I made the team!

Extend: Study the rules for spelling on page 714 in *Write Source*. List three to five words that follow each rule.

© Houghton Mifflin Harcourt Publishing Company

TEKS 9.19
ELPS 5C, 5G

Spelling 2

To become a better speller, study pages 710–714 and pages 716–717 in *Write Source*.

> **Underline** the incorrectly spelled words in the following sentences. Write the corrections above.

1. *phenomenon*
   Hot dogs are an American <u>fenomenom</u>.

2. In 1996, the National Hot Dog and Sausage Counsel sent more than 37,000 wieners to U.S. troops in Bosnia.

3. Busness people know that hot dogs are asocciated with America and good times, which is why you see them in so many advertisements.

4. Even British royalty is aware of the "dog's" extrordinary popularity.

5. President Franklin Roosevelt served Queen Elizabeth II of England hot dogs with potatoe salad at a lunchen.

6. Celebritys like Jerry Seinfeld and Demi Moore promote hot dogs.

7. Hot dogs are the prefered meal when you're in a hurry, since you can hold them in one hand.

8. Hot dogs, on average, wiegh about two ounces.

9. Chili dogs are espesially popular in the Southwest, while southerners favor corn dogs.

10. New Englanders have an appitite for franks and beans, while people from Kansas City find cheese dogs iresistable.

11. Chicagoans load hot dogs with onions, tomatos, pickles, peppers, and a peculier bright-green relish.

12. They call this "draging the dog thorough the garden."

13. What is your favourite way to eat a hot dog?

Extend: Write a mouth-watering description of your favorite hot or cold sandwich. Use words you have trouble spelling. Check your spelling.

© Houghton Mifflin Harcourt Publishing Company

TEKS 9.19
ELPS 5C

Review: Plurals & Spelling

Underline the incorrectly used or misspelled word(s) in each sentence and write the correction above.

1. *reign*
   During the <u>rein</u> of the pharoahs, Egyptians did not consider death the end, but rather the begining of their eternal lifes.

2. They believed that their souls (*bas*) continnued to live on earth, but their spirits (*kas*) traveld back and forth from their bodys to the other world.

3. For this reason, the mummys and the coffins in which they lay were extreemly importent.

4. Canopic jars were placed around the dead pharoahs to hold the brains, tooths, and all internal organes except the haert.

5. A pyramid offered protection aganst weather, decay, and thiefes who might try to steal the objects buried with the body. (Egyptians beleived the *kas* and *bas* used the objects in the afterlife.)

6. Before actual construction could begin on a pyromid, two weeks of prayers and sacrificees were made to the gods.

7. Skilled workers and architectes created the complicated design criteria. They were paid well in food and clotheing.

8. Unskilled workers were used to move millions of stones, some wieghing more than a ton, without horses or donkeyes.

9. Most of the pyramids were constructed of limestone found nearby, but some of the granite had to be shiped from quarrys across the Nile River.

10. Many laborers died from the backbreaking work and unsafe working conditiones.

© Houghton Mifflin Harcourt Publishing Company

 **TEKS** 9.19
ELPS 1C, 4C, 5C

Pretest: Using the Right Word

> **Select** the right word from the choices given in parentheses to complete each sentence.

1. Will you __accept__ this challenge? *(accept, except)*

2. The _____ building is located in our nation's _____ . *(capital, capitol)*

3. Would you _____ me sixty-five cents for bus fare? *(borrow, lend)*

4. Ms. Crawford will _____ us origami in art class. *(learn, teach)*

5. I am _____ to try that spray-on hair color. *(dyeing, dying)*

6. The _____ band attended a picnic following their successful road tour.

   (hole, whole)

7. Dominic asked the teacher, "_____ I please go to the cafeteria?" *(can, may)*

8. The teacher answered, "_____ ." *(all right, alright)*

9. Stay _____ while I make sure this bridge is safe. *(hear, here)*

10. The _____ members soon became _____ by the long report. *(board, bored)*

11. There was _____ too much rain. *(all together, altogether)*

12. The student _____ voted 15–0 in favor of homework limits. *(council, counsel)*

13. After raking a giant pile of leaves, _____ always fun to jump in them. *(it's, its)*

14. Today the wind and the cold kept us from going _____ than two miles.

    (farther, further)

15. Liter bottles are larger _____ quart bottles. *(than, then)*

16. The Chihuahuas continued _____ barking for an hour. *(their, they're)*

17. Are you and _____ cousin camping by Devil's Tower tonight? *(you're, your)*

© Houghton Mifflin Harcourt Publishing Company

 TEKS 9.19
ELPS 1C, 4C, 5C

Using the Right Word 1

Turn to pages 726 and 728 in *Write Source* for help.

> **Write** the correct word above each underlined word that is wrong. If an underlined word is correct, write a *C* above it.

1. This <u>biannual</u> parade is always held on the third Saturday in September.

2. The clowns, who are the crowd favorites, walk <u>among</u> the mayor's car and the high school marching band.

3. The hot sun had a <u>bad</u> <u>affect</u> on one float's fresh flowers.

4. The Jaycees had an amazing float that looked like a desert <u>aisle</u>.

5. The <u>number</u> of parade entries easily exceeded last year's total of 35.

6. One parade watcher said she will gladly <u>adopt</u> to hot weather as long as there is shade along the parade route.

7. All the antique cars <u>except</u> one jalopy were perfectly restored and polished for the car show.

8. The steep <u>assent</u> to the city park marked the end of the parade route.

9. A huge display wall on the back of the final float fell to the pavement and was bent <u>bad</u>.

10. <u>Alot</u> of help was needed to clear the street.

11. Volunteers made sure the float was <u>alright</u> before continuing to the big rally in the park.

12. In spite of the accident, the parade was <u>all together</u> a grand success.

© Houghton Mifflin Harcourt Publishing Company

 TEKS 9.19
ELPS 1C, 4C, 5C

Using the Right Word 2

Turn to pages 730 and 732 in *Write Source* for help.

> Circle the correct word from the pair in parentheses to complete each sentence.

1. In ancient Rome, purple *(die, dye)* for clothing was reserved for emperors.

2. On the other hand, many ordinary Roman citizens often wore *(coarse, course)*, plain cloth.

3. *(Can, May)* you imagine wearing only one kind of clothing?

4. Rome, one of the largest cities of its day, was the *(capital, capitol)* city of the Roman Empire.

5. Roman emperors often sought *(council, counsel)* from their favorite generals.

6. Julius Caesar fought the Gauls when they tried to *(break, brake)* away from Roman rule.

7. During the reign of Trajan, the Roman Empire expanded *(farther, further)* than ever before.

8. Roman generals had their soldiers build numerous roads, walls, and forts to keep them from getting *(board, bored)*.

9. Roman emperors *(cent, sent, scent)* trusted military officers to rule their conquered provinces.

10. The Romans built beautiful structures, but they never built a *(capital, capitol)* building.

© Houghton Mifflin Harcourt Publishing Company

 **TEKS** 9.19
ELPS 1C, 4C, 5B, 5C

Using the Right Word 3

Turn to pages 734 and 736 in *Write Source* for help.

> **Choose** the correct words from the choices given to fill in the blanks in the following story.

1   Allan wanted to help reforest a hillside. He took a special introductory

2   class to _____ how to plant small trees. Allan already knew Mr. Lawson
         (learn, teach)

3   from the high school would _____ the course. Because Allan wanted to
                    (learn, teach)

4   do a _____ job, he listened carefully and took notes. When the instructor
         (good, well)

5   took the class outdoors, Allan practiced using a special tool to make a small

6   _____ in the ground for tree seedlings. To his surprise, Allan found he
    (hole, whole)

7   would be planting trees that were only five inches tall.

8   The next day, Allan was ready to start planting trees. A local tree nursery

9   decided to _____ the class the necessary tools. Allan made a hole and
              (borrow, loan)

10 picked up a _____ tree. Using his _____ , he pushed the
              (healthful, healthy)   *(heal, heel)*

11 soil around the little tree. He smiled because he could _____ people
                                                   (hear, here)

12 humming to themselves. A little bit _____ , Allan started humming, too.
                              (later, latter)

13   When the planting was finished, Allan looked at the small _____
                                                         (medal, meddle)

14 he was given for all of his work. _____ border was gold and _____
                          (it's, its)   *(it's, its)*

15 center showed a tall pine tree. The _____ day he had worked hard, but
                              (hole, whole)

16 he felt good. Before he left the planting site, Allan promised to return _____
                                                              (hear, here)

17 once every year to see how _____ the tiny trees were growing.
                       (good, well)

Extend: Write a sentence for each of the following words: *latter, it's, healthful,* and *borrow.*

© Houghton Mifflin Harcourt Publishing Company

TEKS 9.19
ELPS 1C, 4C, 5B, 5C

Using the Right Word 4

Turn to pages 738 and 740 in *Write Source* for help.

> **Choose** the correct word from column A to fill in the blank in column B.

Column A   **Column B**

miner   **1.** Jill plans to _____ working on this project tonight.

seem   **2.** I have a walk-on role in the third _____ in Act II of the class play.

quiet   **3.** The Fox River runs _____ the county park on the south side of the city.

pour   **4.** Jan _____ the lead runner and surged to victory in the tri-city marathon.

personnel   **5.** The last _____ left on that daisy was "he loves me."

past   **6.** Jane carefully sewed the ripped _____ on Jim's letter jacket.

pore   **7.** A coal _____ works at a dangerous job.

piece   **8.** After midnight, even Main Street becomes very _____.

pedal   **9.** The two old rowboats that those kids are using out on the lake _____ to be sinking!

quit   **10.** The Acre Company expects its _____ to work overtime.

passed   **11.** Every _____ on his forehead bubbled with perspiration as he did pull-ups.

petal   **12.** Compared to the broken water main, this leak was a _____ problem.

seam   **13.** Janae found the missing _____ of the puzzle under the table.

minor   **14.** Jake said the bike's _____ wouldn't move.

scene   **15.** Please _____ this bucket of water in the birdbath.

Extend: Write a sentence for each of the following words: *peace, peddle, personal,* and *quite.*

© Houghton Mifflin Harcourt Publishing Company

 TEKS 9.19
ELPS 1C, 4C, 5C

Using the Right Word 5

Turn to pages 742 and 744 in *Write Source* for help.

> **Choose** the correct word(s) from the choices given to complete each sentence.

1. At one time, car manufacturers in the United States used _____ beams to

make a car's frame. *(steal, steel)*

2. "Remember _____ going to need _____ sleeping bag and _____

backpack for this weekend's campout," Mr. Graham said. *(your, you're)*

3. After studying the cave's small tunnel, Sherman knew he could squeeze

_____ the opening. *(threw, through)*

4. I think the arrows fell over _____, next to that big gray boulder, because

_____ not here. *(their, there, they're)*

5. When Sophie heard I was going hiking, she said, "I want to go, _____."

(to, too, two)

6. People never thought much about garbage, but now _____ management

has become big business. *(waist, waste)*

7. The people on Franklin Street know they will have to _____ a few more

years for their street to be paved. *(wait, weight)*

8. When the bus was ready to leave for the field trip, Mrs. Lane asked,

"_____ missing?" *(who's, whose)*

9. Jack thought he could move the log, but he found out it was heavier _____

he expected. *(than, then)*

10. Mr. Lee, our science teacher, smiled and asked, " Which will _____ more:

a ton of feathers or a ton of bricks?" *(way, weigh)*

© Houghton Mifflin Harcourt Publishing Company

TEKS 9.19
ELPS 1C, 4C, 5C

Review: Using the Right Word

> **Circle** each word that is used incorrectly in the following sentences and write the correct word above it.

1 I went too an air show last week. The sent of jet fuel hung in the air, but

2 I loved it because I want to be a pilot someday. I watched the jets zoom by in

3 formation with the capitol building off in the distance. I could here the engines

4 screaming as the pilots pushed their planes into a steep climb. I wondered how

5 much training the pilots needed to fly those planes.

6 Suddenly, it seemed that the hole sky was full of planes as jets zoomed

7 left and right, while some dove and others climbed. Then, just as suddenly,

8 they were gone. There was a brief moment of piece. The pilots didn't make us

9 weight long; they didn't want us to get board. Quickly, the planes banked and

10 came back. They seamed to be heading right for us. As they zipped passed us,

11 we ducked. Of coarse, we didn't need to do that because the planes weren't that

12 close to us.

13 After the performance was over, I got autographs from some of the

14 pilots. Someone asked me, "Will you borrow me you're pen so I can get some

15 autographs, two?" Latter, one of the pilots talked to me about his plane. "Can I

16 look in the cockpit?" I asked. Wow, some of the gauges were quiet small. There

17 were many switches as well. The pilot told us that his group had to practice alot

18 in order to perform good.

19 When the pilots fly in formation, they must follow the leader. They except

20 his direction as they perform dangerous stunts. The pilots must react quickly.

21 This life-and-death flying leaves no room for performing badly.

© Houghton Mifflin Harcourt Publishing Company

 TEKS 9.19
ELPS 1C, 4C, 5C

22   The pilot I talked to flies an F-16. He said in combat situations the jet can

23   fly further then most fighters. At 32 feet, the wingspan seems to short, but it

24   helps a pilot outmaneuver almost all challengers. Its hard to believe that the

25   F-16 travels at 1,500 miles an hour and reaches an altitude of 50,000 feet. I

26   bought a meddle with the image of the plane on one side and facts about the

27   plane on the other. I learned that the F-16 is about 50 feet long and 16 feet

28   high.

29   I took time to walk between all the jets. I thought about the terrific

30   amount of noise these planes can generate all together. I noticed that red die

31   marked a spot for each nosewheel, and I saw how close they stood to each other.

32   I saw that each jet had the pilot's name on the side to identify who's plane it

33   was. Pilots are pretty particular about there planes because every aircraft

34   handles a bit differently. As I past each plane, I touched a wing or the fuselage.

35   The metal skin felt like steal, but I knew parts of the plane are made of carbon

36   fibers because of their strength and light wait. Still, an F-16 can way as much

37   as 37,500 pounds (which includes the pilot and a full fuel tank) at takeoff.

38   I stepped back and took a picture of the five F-16s along the runway. It

39   was quit a seen. I'll look at it as I study my math and science on my weigh to

40   becoming a pilot.

© Houghton Mifflin Harcourt Publishing Company

TEKS 9.18A, 9.18B, 9.18B(ii)
ELPS 5E

Review: Proofreading Activities

Correct errors in numbers and abbreviations in the following paragraphs. Write the corrections above the errors.

1   The Apollo 13 mission to the moon in 1970 began as planned. Until the

2   movie Apollo Thirteen came out in 1995, many people did not realize what

3   a near tragedy it had been. American astronauts James Lovell, Junior; Fred

4   Haise, JR; and John Swigert, Jr., were launched from Cape Canaveral, Fla., on

5   April eleventh, 1970, for a 10-day mission to land on the moon.

6   One part of their mission was to start an experiment called Apollo

7   Lunar Surface Experiment Package (Alsep). However, fifty-six hours into the

8   flight—about 2 hundred thousand mi. from Earth—an oxygen tank exploded,

9   cutting off all the power in the service module. Unless something could be done

10   quickly, the astronauts would not have enough oxygen to return to Earth. Gene

11   Kranz, the lead flight director in Houston, TX, began working on solutions

12   immediately.

Correct errors in punctuation and capitalization in the following paragraphs. Add any missing punctuation.

1   After the crew shut down a lot of the electrical power they moved from the

2   command module named odyssey, to the lunar module—called aquarius. They

3   were allowed to drink only one glass of water per day. The temperature was

4   near 32 degrees Fahrenheit.

5   Lack of oxygen was the deadliest, most immediate threat. The Aquarius

6   didnt have enough canisters to remove deadly carbon dioxide from the air.

© Houghton Mifflin Harcourt Publishing Company

TEKS 9.18A, 9.18B, 9.18B(ii), 9.18B(iii), 9.19
ELPS 1C, 4C, 5C, 5E

7   The Odyssey did have enough canisters but they were incompatible with the

8   Aquarius system. The engineers in houston, came up with an ingenious

9   solution, they taught the astronauts to create a homemade adapter so the

10   Odyssey canisters could be used on the Aquarius. That solved the oxygen

11   problem.

Correct errors in punctuation and usage in the following paragraphs.

1   The next challenge was to get back home. The astronauts had to use

2   power from the Aquarius to propel their spacecraft, which wayed almost

3   100,000 pounds around the moon and back to Earth. Despite the complexity of

4   this maneuver it was a complete success. The dangerous reentry into Earths

5   atmosphere succeeded, to. On Friday April 17 the crew landed in the Pacific

6   Ocean and were picked up by the navy ship Iwo Jima.

7   The astronauts: Lovell, Haise, and Swigert were heroes. For there bravery,

8   President Richard Nixon awarded them the Metal of Freedom. The men were

9   honored with a parade in Chicago. It would be almost a year before the next

10   lunar mission Apollo 14 would successfully return from the moon on Tuesday

11   February 9 1971.

© Houghton Mifflin Harcourt Publishing Company

Parts of Speech

The activities in this section provide practice and review of the different parts of speech. Most of the activities also include helpful textbook references. In addition, the Extend activities encourage follow-up practice of certain skills.

Nouns **69**

Pronouns **75**

Verbs **89**

Adjectives & Adverbs **107**

Prepositions, Conjunctions, & Interjections **117**

Parts of Speech Review **123**

© Houghton Mifflin Harcourt Publishing Company

Pretest: Nouns

Underline the words used as nouns in the following sentences. Label each noun. Use *P* for proper nouns, *C* for common nouns, and *COL* for collective nouns. Next, circle the abstract nouns and draw a second line under the concrete nouns.

1. Did any American <u>teams</u> *C/COL* win a gold medal at the 2008 Olympic Games in Beijing?

2. Your attitude is a part of your personality.

3. Babe Didrikson Zaharias excelled in track, tennis, golf, and swimming.

4. Jerusalem is a holy city to three religions: Judaism, Islam, and Christianity.

Indicate the functions of each of the underlined nouns in the following sentences. Use these symbols: *S* for subject, *PN* for predicate noun, *IO* for indirect object, *DO* for direct object, and *OP* for object of a preposition. Use *POS* for nouns showing ownership.

_S_ **1.** My little <u>sister</u> reads many books.

_____ **2.** Her favorite book is *Julius, Baby of the World*.

_____ **3.** In this charming <u>children's</u> book, Lilly, the main character, gets a baby <u>brother</u>.

_____ **4.** Lilly is jealous, so she teases her baby <u>brother</u>.

_____ **5.** <u>Lilly's</u> antics are harmless fun.

_____ **6.** My sister laughs aloud when <u>Lilly</u> makes up a story about her <u>brother</u> and says, "Julius was like dust under your bed."

_____ **7.** Then her cousin makes insulting remarks about <u>Julius</u>.

_____ **8.** Lilly immediately gives <u>Julius</u> her love.

© Houghton Mifflin Harcourt Publishing Company

TEKS 9.13C
ELPS 4C

Classes of Nouns 1

A noun is a word that names something: a person, a place, a thing, or an idea. There are five classes of nouns: *proper, common, concrete, abstract,* and *collective.* Turn to 747.1–747.5 in *Write Source.*

Underline the words used as nouns in the following summary. Identify the nouns using *P* for a proper noun, *C* for a common noun, and *COL* for a collective noun. (Collective nouns will have a double classification: *P/COL* or *C/COL*.)

                                  P   C   C   C

1   The <u>Constitution</u>, a <u>document</u> that has played an important <u>role</u> in <u>history</u>,

                                      C   C   P/COL

2   clearly defines the <u>freedoms</u> and <u>goals</u> of the <u>United States of America</u>. It was

3   written in Philadelphia at the Constitutional Convention. Fifty-five

4   representatives from a dozen states drafted the document between May and

5   September of 1787. George Washington was chosen as president of the

6   convention, which included such statesmen as James Madison, Benjamin

7   Franklin, and Alexander Hamilton. Because of his role in the convention, and

8   his ability to resolve disputes, James Madison became known as the Father of

9   the Constitution. Governor Morris of Pennsylvania was responsible for the

10   expressive literary style of the Constitution—an unusual feature for an official

11   document. The convention was in session for 16 weeks. These weeks included

12   many trying days and nights. Some of the delegates even withdrew at one

13   point, claiming that the convention was overstepping its authority by drafting a

14   constitution.

List the nouns from the first sentence in the paragraph above on the correct lines below. (There should be three concrete nouns and four abstract nouns.)

concrete: _____

abstract: _____

Extend: Study a paragraph from your writing. Underline the nouns. Read "Specific Nouns" on page 586 in *Write Source.* Could you have used more vivid nouns?

© Houghton Mifflin Harcourt Publishing Company

TEKS 9.18A
ELPS 4C

Classes of Nouns 2

Proper nouns are always capitalized. Common nouns are not capitalized. Abstract nouns name ideas or feelings, while concrete nouns name tangible things. Learn more about the classes of nouns to improve your writing. Turn to page 747 in *Write Source*.

Complete each pair below with either a proper or a common noun. Use capitalization as needed. Remember to underline the titles of movies and books.

PROPER	COMMON
1. Tom Hanks	*actor*
2. *Central Park*	park
3. _____	president
4. _____	movie
5. Oklahoma	_____
6. _____	book
7. _____	religion
8. Spain	_____

Make a list of abstract nouns and concrete nouns.

ABSTRACT	CONCRETE
1. _____	1. _____
2. _____	2. _____
3. _____	3. _____
4. _____	4. _____
5. _____	5. _____
6. _____	6. _____
7. _____	7. _____
8. _____	8. _____

© Houghton Mifflin Harcourt Publishing Company

ELPS 4C, 5E

Functions of Nouns

Nouns can be used six different ways. Study the chart below and turn to 748.3 in *Write Source* for more information.

Write Source	Function	Symbol	Example
780.1	subject	**S**	*Pilots* fly.
748.3, 758.1	predicate	**PN**	Pilots are *captains*.
760.2	direct object	**DO**	Pilots fly *planes*.
760.2	indirect object	**IO**	The pilot gave *passengers* a message.
776	object of preposition	**OP**	The pilot spoke to the *people*.
748.3	possessive noun	**POS**	The pilot got the *passengers'* attention.

> **Identify** how the underlined nouns function in the following statements, using the symbols from the chart above.

1. *S* Birds have *DO* eyes on the *OP* sides of their heads.

2. A group of lions is a pride.

3. A lion's pride is often his mane.

4. The name for a group of monkeys is a band.

5. Only female mosquitoes bite.

6. The ostrich is the largest bird; it is also the fastest runner.

7. The smallest bird is the bee hummingbird; it weighs less than a penny.

8. Loons, the fastest swimmers, can also dive 160 feet below the surface.

9. A loon can outswim fish and catch them underwater.

10. Loons are shy birds; and their haunting calls give some people goose bumps.

11. Geese, the highest flyers, have been known to fly at 29,000 feet.

12. A peregrine falcon can dive at a speed of 200 miles per hour.

13. The curlew, a long-legged bird related to the sandpiper, can fly 2,000 miles

nonstop over water.

Extend: Write four to six sentences about your favorite animals. Include nouns in each sentence; try to use at least three of the six functions listed in the chart above.

© Houghton Mifflin Harcourt Publishing Company

ELPS 4C

Nominative, Possessive, & Objective Cases of Nouns

To determine the case of a noun, look at the way it is used in the sentence. Study the chart below before turning to 748.3 in *Write Source*.

Write Source	Case	Function	Symbol	Example
780.1	*Nominative*	*subject*	**S**	The *car* wouldn't start.
748.3		*predicate noun*	**PN**	The car is a *lemon*.
760.2	*Objective*	*direct object*	**DO**	Jake's driving gives me the *creeps*.
760.2		*indirect object*	**IO**	Jake's driving gives *Hannah* the creeps.
776		*object of preposition*	**OP**	He drives with one *hand*.
748.3	*Possessive*	*possessive noun*	**POS**	*Hannah's* driving skills are much better.

Label the function of the underlined nouns in the following statements using the symbols from the chart above. Indicate the case of each underlined noun (*N* for nominative, *O* for objective, and *POS* for possessive) on the blanks.

___N___   *S*
1. Dolphins are aquatic mammals related to both whales and porpoises.

_____ **2.** These amazing creatures live in seas and rivers all over the world.

_____ **3.** Measuring less than four feet, the *buffeo* is the smallest dolphin known.

_____ **4.** Most dolphins eat nearly one-third of their weight in food every day.

_____ **5.** For years, humans hunted dolphins for their valuable oil.

_____ **6.** Considering their fragile history, the dolphins' survival is remarkable.

_____ **7.** Between 1959 and 1972, an estimated 4.8 million dolphins were killed when they became entangled in tuna fishing nets.

_____ **8.** Then, the United States threw dolphins a lifeline and helped stop the tragedy.

_____ **9.** It pressured both domestic and international tuna canneries to refuse shipments from fleets that did not protect dolphins.

_____ **10.** The United States passed the Marine Mammal Protection Act of 1972.

_____ **11.** It prevents the exploitation of aquatic animals, including dolphins.

© Houghton Mifflin Harcourt Publishing Company

ELPS 4C, 5E

Review: Nouns

Make lists by filling in the following blanks with the types of nouns called for in the headings. For ideas, think about something that interests you, such as camping, sports, or a subject you're studying.

Proper Nouns

1. _____
2. _____
3. _____

Common Nouns

1. _____
2. _____
3. _____

Collective Nouns

1. _____
2. _____
3. _____

Abstract Nouns

1. _____
2. _____
3. _____

Concrete Nouns

1. _____
2. _____

Write two sentences using some of the nouns you've listed. (Try to use at least one noun from each of your lists.) Underline and label the nouns in your sentences; use *NOM* for nominative case, *OBJ* for objective case, and *POS* for possessive case.

1. _____

_____

2. _____

_____

© Houghton Mifflin Harcourt Publishing Company

ELPS 4C

Pretest: Pronouns

> **Underline** all of the pronouns in the following sentences. Then label each pronoun **S** for singular or **P** for plural.

1. We talked all night about videos and music.

2. She studied John Steinbeck's *Of Mice and Men.*

3. Walking along the beach, they saw starfish washed up on the shore.

4. If he eats burritos or other spicy foods before bedtime, his nightmares return.

5. If you don't watch what you are doing, you will hurt yourself.

6. I like my peas on one side of my plate and my carrots on the other side of

my plate.

7. Many of the football players wanted their coach to go for a first down.

8. The car had a hole in its radiator.

9. Mardi Gras is also called "Fat Tuesday" because for some people it is the last

day to eat certain foods before their Lenten fasting begins.

> **Underline** all of the pronouns in the following sentences. Then label each pronoun with its case (**N** for nominative, **POS** for possessive, or **O** for objective).

      N   *POS*   *O*
1. She took all our towels with her to the beach.

2. Our neighbors' dog is constantly digging up their lawn.

3. We wish they would keep it on a leash.

4. Their motorcycle wouldn't fit onto its trailer.

5. Either you or I can get the catcher's mitt later.

6. Did anybody see what happened to his car?

7. I told them that they were too late.

© Houghton Mifflin Harcourt Publishing Company

ELPS 4C, 5E

Types of Pronouns

There are three different types of pronouns: simple, compound, and phrasal. Turn to page 750 in *Write Source*.

> **When Martin Luther King, Jr., was born, *he* was destined to be a great man.**
> (The pronoun *he* is simple.)

> **King knew that people had to believe in *themselves*.**
> (The pronoun *themselves* is compound)

> **King also wanted people to love *one another*.**
> (The pronoun *one another* is phrasal.)

Underline the pronouns in the sentences below. Study the first pronoun in each sentence. In the blank write an *S* if the pronoun is simple, a *C* if it is compound, and a *P* if it is phrasal.

P **1.** Martin Luther King's dream was to have a world where people lived with <u>each</u> <u>other</u> in peace.

_____ **2.** Everybody who has heard King's brilliant "I Have a Dream" speech is inspired.

_____ **3.** Long before honor and fame found him, King worked as well as dreamed.

_____ **4.** After successfully organizing a bus boycott in 1956, he became a leader in the civil rights movement.

_____ **5.** Martin Luther King studied the practices of Mahatma Gandhi, and King himself followed nonviolent civil disobedience.

_____ **6.** In 1960 King accepted a co-pastorship with his father at Ebenezer Baptist Church in Atlanta.

_____ **7.** In 1964 *Time* magazine chose King as Man of the Year, the first black American it had thus honored.

Extend: Write four or five sentences about a famous (or not-so-famous) person. Use at least one pronoun per sentence. Exchange papers with a classmate. Underline and identify the types of pronouns.

© Houghton Mifflin Harcourt Publishing Company

ELPS 2D, 2I, 3E, 3F, 4C, 4G, 4F

Personal Pronouns

A pronoun takes the place of a noun or nouns. By correctly using pronouns, you can avoid repetition and write smoother, more readable sentences. Turn to 750.1 in *Write Source* for the chart "Classes of Pronouns."

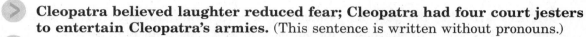

> **Cleopatra believed laughter reduced fear; Cleopatra had four court jesters to entertain Cleopatra's armies.** (This sentence is written without pronouns.)

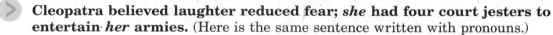

> **Cleopatra believed laughter reduced fear; *she* had four court jesters to entertain *her* armies.** (Here is the same sentence written with pronouns.)

Replace the underlined nouns in the following narrative with the appropriate pronouns.

1   Cleopatra, who ruled Egypt from 47 B.C.E. to 30 B.C.E., enjoyed luxury.
                 she   *her*

2   For example, <u>Cleopatra</u> had four court jesters to make <u>Cleopatra</u> laugh and to

3   entertain <u>Cleopatra's</u> armies. <u>Cleopatra</u> was rich, extravagant, and demanding.

4   Slaves quickly obeyed <u>Cleopatra's</u> every order. Cleopatra demanded that <u>slaves</u>

5   fill <u>Cleopatra's</u> bathtub with milk every day. Cleopatra believed the milk kept

6   <u>Cleopatra's</u> skin soft. <u>Cleopatra</u> also worried about <u>Cleopatra's</u> complexion.

7   One of the legends about Cleopatra demonstrates <u>Cleopatra's</u> concern. The

8   legend says that <u>Cleopatra</u> once dissolved a large, lustrous pearl in a glass

9   of vinegar. <u>Cleopatra</u> did this in front of many guests at a banquet.

10   <u>Cleopatra's guests</u> were astonished! And <u>Cleopatra's guests</u> were even more

11   surprised when Cleopatra drank the mixture. <u>The mixture</u> was supposed

12   to ensure a lustrous complexion. The legends about Cleopatra's riches and

13   extravagance are endless. Some of <u>the legends</u> are true; others are mere myth.

Extend: Select a passage from a book or magazine. Exchange passages with a classmate and take turns reading them aloud. Whenever a pronoun is used, don't read it aloud; pause and ask the listener to supply it. If your classmate has trouble naming the pronoun, tell him or her the antecedent. This exercise requires careful listening and comprehension monitoring (making sure that you understand what you hear).

© Houghton Mifflin Harcourt Publishing Company

ELPS 4C

Number & Person of Personal Pronouns

The *number* of a pronoun can be either singular or plural. The *person* of a pronoun shows who is speaking (first person), who is spoken to (second person), or who is spoken about (third person). Turn to 754.1–754.2 in *Write Source* for more information.

> **Underline** all of the personal pronouns in the following sentences. Then label each pronoun. Use *S* for singular and *P* for plural. Use *1, 2,* and *3* for first, second, and third person. Label "you" *S-P* when it can be either singular or plural.

          P/1   S-P/2

1. What makes us laugh? How would you define laughter?

2. A comedian once said, "I can't define laughter, but I know it when I feel it."

3. "It is like a 'happy spasm,'" he added.

4. Doctors and psychiatrists say laughter is good for us.

5. It stimulates our hearts, increases our circulation, and exercises our stomach and chest muscles.

6. Research has proven it helps our immune system by increasing the number of cells that we need for healing and fighting disease.

7. I did some research of my own.

8. I asked each of my classmates, "How many times do you laugh each day?"

9. When you were in kindergarten, you probably laughed as many as 300 times a day.

10. By the time we become adults, we laugh only about 15 times daily.

11. Laughter is one of the things that makes your life, and mine, worth living.

12. Another writer took this view: "We laugh in order not to cry."

Extend: Write a joke or an anecdote that makes you laugh. Share your writing with a classmate. When you're done laughing, locate the personal pronouns in each piece. Tell each other the number and person for each.

© Houghton Mifflin Harcourt Publishing Company

ELPS 4C

Functions of Pronouns

Pronouns function in the same way that nouns do. Study the chart below and turn to 710.1 in *Write Source*.

Write Source	Function	Symbol	Example
780.1	*subject*	**S**	*You* need to change your clothes.
756.1	*predicate nominative*	**PN**	"That is *you*," she remarked about my shirt.
760.2	*direct object*	**DO**	The river's current pulled *him* under.
760.2	*indirect object*	**IO**	Frank gave *me* some paperback books.
776	*object of preposition*	**OP**	This isn't about *me*.
756.1	*possessive noun*	**POS**	*His* shoes were ruined by the rain.

Identify how the underlined pronouns function in the following statements, using the symbols from the chart above.

 S   POS
1. Some of the little children lost their coats while on the field trip.

2. They were engrossed with the exhibit and forgot about them.

3. Their teachers helped look for the lost coats.

4. "I know where my coat is," said Sam.

5. "I left it on the bus," he said.

6. "My lunch is lost," cried a little girl.

7. "She lost her lunch," a little boy said.

8. "Will you do me a favor?" the bus driver asked.

9. He asked her to sit quietly while he went to the bus and got her lunch.

10. "They are so cute," their teacher said.

11. The bus driver nodded his head.

12. "They love field trips," another teacher added.

13. "Did you find it," the little girl asked the bus driver.

14. "Yes, I did," he said.

15. "I am one of the children who likes you," the little girl said.

© Houghton Mifflin Harcourt Publishing Company

ELPS 4C, 5E

Nominative, Possessive, & Objective Cases of Pronouns 1

The case of a personal pronoun is determined by how that pronoun is used within a sentence. Is the pronoun being used as a subject, an object, or a possessive? Turn to 756.1 in *Write Source* for more information and a chart that identifies the case for each pronoun.

> **Write** the case for each pronoun listed below. Use *N* for nominative, *POS* for possessive, and *O* for objective. Watch for pronouns that have more than one case.

_N___ **1.** I   _____ **6.** theirs   _____ **11.** its   _____ **16.** them

_____ **2.** we   _____ **7.** mine   _____ **12.** you   _____ **17.** me

_____ **3.** she   _____ **8.** they   _____ **13.** their   _____ **18.** it

_____ **4.** our   _____ **9.** he   _____ **14.** his   _____ **19.** my

_____ **5.** her   _____ **10.** him   _____ **15.** hers   _____ **20.** us

> **Add** the missing pronoun to each of the sentences below as called for in parentheses.

1. ___We___ are going. *(1st person plural, nominative)*

2. _____ am going. *(1st person singular, nominative)*

3. She and _____ are going, too. *(3rd person singular, nominative)*

4. I asked Ed and Juan, "Are _____ joining us?" *(2nd person plural, nominative)*

5. _____ said no. *(3rd person plural, nominative)*

6. _____ decision is final. *(1st person plural, possessive)*

7. _____ heart is sad. *(1st person singular, possessive)*

8. _____ heart rate has slowed. *(3rd person singular, possessive)*

9. We must leave without _____ . *(3rd person plural, objective)*

10. Do you think _____ car is big enough? *(2nd person plural, possessive)*

Extend: Write eight to ten sentences using pronouns from the exercises above. Exchange papers with a classmate. Read each other's sentences to see if the pronouns are used correctly.

© Houghton Mifflin Harcourt Publishing Company

ELPS 4C

Nominative, Possessive, & Objective Cases of Pronouns 2

A pronoun can show ownership (possessive case). A pronoun can also act as a subject (nominative case) or as an object of a verb or preposition (objective case). For more information on pronouns, turn to 756.1 in *Write Source*.

> **Underline** the pronouns in the sentences below. Label the case for each pronoun. Use *N* for nominative, *POS* for possessive, and *O* for objective.

             N   *O*

1. Most of us know something about tropical rain forests.

2. We know their plant and animal life is being destroyed.

3. But did you know there are other kinds of tropical forests?

4. Have you and your classmates heard about cloud forests?

5. They are also called tropical montane forests. ("Montane" means mountain.)

6. Each of the forests survives under its own special weather conditions.

7. Even though I have never seen one, a cloud forest seems as fascinating to me as a rain forest.

8. My biology teacher, Ms. Green, has studied plant life at Costa Rica's Monteverde Cloud Forest.

9. The forest is located on top of a mountain range known as the Cordillera de Tilaran; Ms. Green says it is bathed in clouds almost every day.

10. A botanist, who has been studying the Monteverde Cloud Forest for 20 years, was her supervisor and mentor.

11. Ms. Green learned a great deal there, and our class will benefit from her experience.

Extend: Read the second paragraph of the essay on page 89 in this *SkillsBook*. Make a list of the personal pronouns you find. Identify the case for each pronoun.

© Houghton Mifflin Harcourt Publishing Company

ELPS 3D, 3F–3H, 4C

Pronoun Cases: *I* and *Me*

When do you use "I" and when do you use "me"? Do you get confused when it comes to using *I* and *me?* Turn to 756.1 in *Write Source.*

Pronouns make my eyeballs blur–
He and *she, him* and *her,*
She and *I, me* and *him–*
My poor noggin starts to swim.

Subject, object what to do?
Here's a rhyme to help you through,
He can go with *her* and *me*
If *she* and *I* go to the sea.

Pronouns change case depending on how they are used in a sentence. There are three cases: nominative (used as subjects), objective (used as indirect and direct objects, or objects of prepositions) and possessive (used to indicate ownership).
Two pronouns that can cause trouble are *I* and *me.*

Choose the correct pronouns in the sentences below.

1. Both he and *(I, me)* are determined to learn to speak and write well.

2. Our teachers offered him and *(I, me)* recommendations.

3. Both my mother and *(I, me)* wanted to dance with Dad.

4. My cat plays more than *(I, me).*

5. Ceci and *(I, me)* ate all the dill pickles.

6. Thank you for giving Philip and *(I, me)* a ride to work.

7. Just between you and *(I, me),* I think he's a good friend.

8. Mother wanted to dance more than *(I, me).*

9. Niles found out that Julio and *(I, me)* are twins.

10. Do you want to go with *(I, me)*?

Extend: Using your knowledge about nominative and objective cases (in other words, about using subjects and objects), explain to a classmate why you chose each pronoun. When you disagree, use your handbooks to find information that will help you reach agreement about which pronoun is correct.

© Houghton Mifflin Harcourt Publishing Company

ELPS 4C

Review: Pronouns 1

> **Label** the underlined pronouns either *N* for nominative case, *O* for objective case, or *POS* for possessive case. On the first blank at the left, indicate the number of each pronoun. Use *S* for singular and *P* for plural. On the second blank, indicate the person of each pronoun. Use *1*, *2*, and *3* to indicate first, second, and third person.

_P_ _3_   **1.** Chen and Sarah are not sure <u>they</u> should see the new movie.   *N* (above "they")

___ ___   **2.** Why do you want to go with <u>us</u>?

___ ___   **3.** The teacher said that <u>they</u> should read 25 pages a day.

___ ___   **4.** When will <u>she</u> come to the house to fix the pipe leak downstairs?

___ ___   **5.** Megan and Kevin, <u>you</u> need to find another member for the group.

___ ___   **6.** Shannon thinks that the ring she found on the floor is <u>yours</u>.

___ ___   **7.** Frank thinks that <u>he</u> would like to go to the mall instead of

the coffeehouse.

___ ___   **8.** Jake, what do <u>you</u> think the class should do to help

the environment?

___ ___   **9.** The cat wanted <u>his</u> food immediately.

___ ___ **10.** I feel as bad as <u>she</u> does.

___ ___ **11.** That's what she and <u>I</u> would like to know.

___ ___ **12.** Margaret and <u>they</u> are going on a field trip.

___ ___ **13.** Mr. Hatcher gave Mishka and <u>me</u> permission.

___ ___ **14.** Let's keep it between you and <u>me</u>.

___ ___ **15.** Reba reminded <u>them</u> about the cost of concert tickets.

___ ___ **16.** Do you want to come along with <u>him</u>?

___ ___ **17.** The car wouldn't start because <u>its</u> battery was dead.

___ ___ **18.** They knew it was <u>my</u> dog.

___ ___ **19.** Nobody hits the bull's-eye more than <u>I</u>.

© Houghton Mifflin Harcourt Publishing Company

ELPS 4C, 5B, 5E, 5G

Reflexive & Intensive Pronouns

Reflexive and intensive pronouns are formed by adding -self or -selves to personal pronouns (*myself, yourselves*). An intensive pronoun is a reflexive pronoun that emphasizes the noun or pronoun it refers to. Turn to 750.1 and 752.1 in *Write Source*.

> **Choose** the correct reflexive or intensive pronoun in each sentence below. On the blank to the left, indicate with an *R* or an *I* whether the pronoun is reflexive or intensive.

_____ **1.** The group of four called (*themselves,* himself) the "Rowdy Band of Four."

_____ **2.** Mrs. Wenchley (*ourself, herself*) came to our final rehearsal to lend her full support.

_____ **3.** After Maurice found the stolen items, he returned them (*himself, themselves*) to the band.

_____ **4.** I couldn't help but think to (*myself, himself*) what an awesome job Jason had done in promoting the event.

_____ **5.** Demetrius and Tanya worked (*ourselves, themselves*) to a point of near exhaustion to make sure everything was ready for the next day.

_____ **6.** Rallying behind our courageous leader, we stepped onto stage to find (*ourselves, themselves*) surrounded by a nearly full arena.

_____ **7.** Oddly enough, it was Paul (*himself, myself*) who stepped to the microphone to quiet the crowd.

_____ **8.** As the music continued, time (*itself, itselves*) seemed to stand still.

_____ **9.** All our efforts were rewarded when the crowd continued to applaud louder and longer than we (*ourself, ourselves*) had ever dreamed possible.

Extend: Write a paragraph explaining the difference between reflexive and intensive pronouns, including specific examples of each type of pronoun.

© Houghton Mifflin Harcourt Publishing Company

TEKS 9.17A(iii)
ELPS 3D, 3E, 3G, 4C

Reciprocal Pronouns

Reciprocal pronouns refer to the individual members of a plural antecedent and express mutual action or relationship. The two reciprocal pronouns in English are *each other* and *one another*. Traditional guidelines recommend that *each other* be used in reference to two individuals, while *one another* be used in reference to more than two. Turn to 750.1 and 752.3 in *Write Source*.

Write the recommended reciprocal pronoun (*each other* or *one another*) in each sentence below.

1. Your neighbors trickled out of their homes, looking at _____ in amazement at the storm's damage.

2. Juan and Anna called _____ to plan a meeting of the neighborhood council.

3. Several people joined the meeting to suggest ways that we could come together as a community to assist _____ with clean up efforts.

4. While the schools were closed, the teachers worked with _____ to get their classrooms ready for students to return.

5. After schools reopened, Paul and I discussed with _____ the astonishing ways the whole community had united to help us through a difficult time.

6. I hope our community never sees another storm like that one, but if we do, I'm certain that everyone in our community will join forces to help _____.

Extend: Discuss with a partner your feelings about a time when you and your friends accomplished something special or worked together to meet a challenge. Use both reciprocal pronouns in your conversation.

© Houghton Mifflin Harcourt Publishing Company

TEKS 9.17A(ii)
ELPS 4C, 5B, 5E, 5G

Relative Pronouns

A relative pronoun (*that, who, whom, whose, which*) relates an adjective clause to the noun or pronoun it modifies ("He *who* hesitates misses opportunities."). Turn to 750.1 and 752.2 in *Write Source*.

> **Underline** the relative pronoun in each of the sentences below. Circle the noun or pronoun that it modifies.

1. Carnivorous (plants,) <u>which</u> eat insects and other animals, live mainly in marshy areas.

2. Venus flytrap, a bog plant that grows in the Southeast, is the most famous carnivore.

3. Botanists who study carnivorous species have found that the plants need minerals from their prey to survive.

4. Most carnivorous plants eat insects and arthropods, but some have also been known to eat slugs and frogs, which are also nutritious.

5. Carnivorous plants have three different methods of trapping, which determine their appearance.

6. The so-called *pitfalls*, which have tubular leaves, use a water-filled pit to catch insects.

7. Some carnivorous plants use a sticky substance to trap their dinner—insects that are unfortunate enough to get too close.

8. Finally, the third group of plants, which includes Venus flytraps, actually move their leaves to enclose their prey and then slowly digest it.

9. Usually the Venus flytrap, whose leaves are like jaws, will close a trap after it has caught three insects in it.

Extend: Write the beginning of a descriptive essay. Include specific sensory details, and use relative pronouns correctly.

© Houghton Mifflin Harcourt Publishing Company

ELPS 2D, 2I, 3E, 3F, 4C, 5B, 5E

Indefinite, Interrogative, & Demonstrative Pronouns

Indefinite pronouns represent someone (or something) not specifically named or known (*many, anyone, nobody*). Demonstrative pronouns point out a specific person or a specific thing (for example, *This* is my brother, John). Interrogative pronouns are used in questions (*who? which? what?*). Turn to 750.1 and 752.4–752.6 in *Write Source*.

> **Identify** the pronouns underlined in the sentences below. Use *IND* for indefinite, *DEM* for demonstrative, and *INT* for interrogative.

1   Many historians think the people who invented numbers lived in the Arab

2   world about 5,000 years ago. Yet <u>nobody</u> knows for certain who used numbers

3   first. <u>Which</u> of the ancient cultures had the greatest need for numbers? Our

4   answers may indicate who "invented" them.

5   For instance, <u>who</u> built the pyramids? <u>Who</u> built the Great Wall of China?

6   <u>Somebody</u> probably needed numbers to build these projects. And what about

7   taxes? Even long ago, almost <u>everyone</u> had to pay them. How did the tax

8   collectors keep track of who had paid and <u>who</u> had not? Is <u>that</u> why people

9   invented a numeral system?

10   In the current century, <u>who</u> could go through a day without numbers?

11 Almost <u>everyone</u> learns about numbers at an early age. <u>Most</u> of us can hold up

12 two fingers to show our age when we are two years old. <u>That</u> may be the first

13 way we learn to use numbers today. <u>Everybody</u> uses numbers in some way;

14 <u>these</u> are technological times.

15   <u>Who</u> invented numbers? Though we don't really know for sure, we know

16 that <u>whoever</u> it was changed the course of history.

Extend: Choose several indefinite, interrogative, and demonstrative pronouns from the chart on page 750 in *Write Source*. Write a sentence for each pronoun you select. Then read your sentences and direct a classmate to identify the pronouns, and then switch roles.

© Houghton Mifflin Harcourt Publishing Company

ELPS 4C

Review: Pronouns 2

> **Underline** and label the pronouns in the sentences below. Use *P* for personal, *R* for relative, *I* for indefinite, *INT* for interrogative, *DEM* for demonstrative, and *RX* for reflexive.

1. The general tried to help <u>his</u> daughter.
   P

2. Joe can keep himself company.

3. The boy who went home early should still do his part.

4. That is not enough money for Kate to buy flowers.

5. Everyone needs to help put the equipment away in the storage closet.

6. Katia, who went to the store, bought ripe strawberries.

7. Sally said she had to go home to do the dishes and fold laundry.

8. The science report that was under the couch was due last week.

9. Those are the shoes that Moira wears to school.

10. Many went to Yellowstone National Park to see the geysers.

11. That doesn't look like banana bread!

12. Father asked Joni a question, but she didn't hear him.

13. To whom did Mike give the pencil?

14. Some families take their pets with them when they travel.

15. Aaron takes himself too seriously.

16. Mr. and Mrs. Wateri gave away their used books.

17. "Sarah, where did you get that?"

18. "Please, get out of my way," the janitor said.

19. Who caught the runaway gerbil?

20. Give yourself credit for doing well on this review!

© Houghton Mifflin Harcourt Publishing Company

ELPS 4C

Pretest: Verbs

> **Circle** all of the verbs in the following paragraphs. (Be sure not to circle any verbals.)

1   Creative writing is the best class! We try to activate all of our senses.
2   One day our teacher gave us gelatin cubes. We looked at them, felt them,
3   smelled them, bounced them, tasted them. Perry Thompson pretended to have
4   a conversation with his cube after he named it Ebenezer. Some days we go
5   for a walk around the school or through the halls in order to use all our senses.
6   Mrs. Zechel's home economics class invited us to tea. That required all our
7   senses and our best manners.
8   Each week we get an anthology of our writings: the best satire, the best
9   poem, the best sentence, a list of the best strong nouns and verbs, the piece
10   with the best sentence variety, a list of the most common errors, and so forth.
11   Our teacher writes comments on all these pieces; these comments are useful.
12   We can all discover what she sees in our writing. Some days we write to music.
13   We read some of our best writings at the local coffee shop several evenings
14   throughout the semester. Once a week we measure our fluency by printing on
15   a banner and then measuring the length of the banner. Last week I wrote
16   seven feet! I am learning a lot in creative writing. The writing practice is good
17   for me.

> **Provide** the following information from the paragraph above.

1. List two linking verbs. _____

2. List two auxiliary (helping) verbs. _____

3. List five past tense verbs. _____

_____

4. List six present tense verbs. _____

_____

5. In your opinion, what is the strongest verb in the paragraph? _____

6. List an irregular verb. _____

© Houghton Mifflin Harcourt Publishing Company

90

TEKS 9.13C
ELPS 4C

Types of Verbs

A verb is a word that expresses action (*started, declare, ran*) or state of being (*is, are, am*). In this exercise, you will identify action verbs. You probably remember that some action verbs have helping verbs. They have already been underlined in the following narrative. Turn to page 758 and index number 760.1 in *Write Source*.

Underline the action verbs in the following narrative. (Do not underline verbals.)

1 The era of the steam railroad in America <u>started</u> on a Saturday morning in

2 August, 1829, in the forest of eastern Pennsylvania. There Horatio Allen, a

3 bright, twenty-seven-year-old civil engineer and recent graduate of Columbia

4 College, introduced the country to the "Stourbridge Lion," a seven-ton

5 locomotive. Using the "Lion" as his test vehicle, Allen hoped to prove the

6 potential of steam-driven engines as an efficient means of mass transportation.

7 For the test, the locomotive <u>was</u> driven across nearby Lackawaxen Creek on a

8 makeshift wooden trestle that formed a curve nearly a quarter of a mile long.

9 The many eager onlookers believed that the locomotive known as the "iron

10 monster" <u>would</u> either collapse the trestle or jump the track at the curve, go

11 over the edge, and plunge into the creek thirty feet below. Risking no life but

12 his own, Allen, the future president of the Erie Railroad, climbed aboard the

13 "Lion," took the throttle, started down the track, and made the six-mile run

14 without mishap. Despite the success, the "Stourbridge Lion" <u>was</u> declared too

15 heavy for its tracks. It <u>was</u> put into storage and later used for parts. But this

16 one short run opened the way for future railroads to play a vital role in the

17 settlement and development of America.

(Did you find 17 verbs?)

Extend: Study a piece of your own writing. Underline the verbs. After reading about specific verbs on page 590 in *Write Source,* replace any weak verbs in your writing. Do you find any verbs in the above narrative that could be more vivid? If so, write your choice above the verb you would replace.

© Houghton Mifflin Harcourt Publishing Company

ELPS 4C, 5E

Auxiliary (Helping) & Linking Verbs

Linking verbs describe a "state of being." They simply tell us how someone or something is (or tastes, feels, looks, and so forth). Turn to 758.1 in *Write Source* for a list of linking verbs. Auxiliary verbs are "helpers." They are added to main verbs to form the perfect tenses and the passive voice. Turn to 758.2 in *Write Source*.

> **Underline** each linking verb or auxiliary verb in the sentences below. On the blanks provided, write **A** for the auxiliary verbs and **L** for the linking verbs.

A   **1.** Julius Caesar was born on July 12th or 13th in approximately 100 B.C.E.

_____   **2.** Never before had Rome experienced an emperor of Caesar's military and political ability.

_____   **3.** In his early life, Caesar was a military commander for part of the Roman empire.

_____   **4.** Caesar was gaining political strength and popularity during this time.

_____   **5.** He looked like a strong leader.

_____   **6.** After Caesar had turned against Pompey—once his ally—he gained significant power.

_____   **7.** He may have turned against Pompey for the good of Rome or for personal gain.

_____   **8.** In 44 B.C.E., Caesar was crowned dictator for life.

_____   **9.** But a number of prominent Romans were plotting against Caesar.

_____   **10.** Brutus and other conspirators had plotted to kill Caesar on March 15, 44 B.C.E.

_____   **11.** Brutus, once Caesar's friend, eventually became his worst enemy.

Extend: Write four or five sentences about a historical figure, using both linking and auxiliary verbs. Underline and label the linking and auxiliary verbs in the sentences you write.

© Houghton Mifflin Harcourt Publishing Company

ELPS 4C, 5E

Present, Past, & Future Tense Verbs

Writers use verb tenses to indicate time. The present tense of a verb states an action that is happening now or regularly. The past tense of a verb states an action that happened at a specific time in the past. The future tense of a verb states an action that will take place in the future. Turn to 762.3–762.4 in *Write Source*.

> **Rewrite** the sentence in each group below using the tenses indicated. Keep the meaning of the sentences as close as possible to that of the original.

1. *Present:* ___Making a movie involves many people.___

Past: Making a movie involved many people.

Future: ___Making a movie will involve many people.___

2. *Present:* _____

Past: First, a screenwriter wrote a script.

Future: _____

3. *Present:* _____

Past: _____

Future: Next, the casting director will pick the actors.

4. *Present:* Then the crew builds the sets.

Past: _____

Future: _____

5. *Present:* _____

Past: _____

Future: The director and editors will assemble the final film.

6. *Present:* _____

Past: Finally, you watched the movie while you ate your popcorn.

Future: _____

Extend: Choose a short passage from a history book and rewrite it in the future tense.

© Houghton Mifflin Harcourt Publishing Company

TEKS 9.17A(i)
ELPS 4C, 5E

Perfect Tense Verbs

It may take some practice, but you can understand verb tenses perfectly. Like simple tenses, perfect tenses deal with time. To learn about perfect tenses, turn to 764.1 in *Write Source*. Also refer to the past participles for irregular verbs on that page.

> **Write** the past participle for each of the present tense verbs listed below. Then, write the verb in the perfect tense indicated in the parentheses.

Present Tense	Past Participle		Perfect Tense of the Verb
1. be	*been*	*(present perfect):*	*has been* (or) *have been*
2. fly		*(future perfect):*	
3. show		*(present perfect):*	
4. take		*(past perfect):*	
5. ride		*(future perfect):*	
6. run		*(past perfect):*	
7. drag		*(present perfect):*	
8. lay		*(future perfect):*	
9. swim		*(past perfect):*	
10. choose		*(future perfect):*	
11. go		*(past perfect):*	
12. see		*(present perfect):*	
13. shine		*(present perfect):*	
14. freeze		*(past perfect):*	
15. give		*(future perfect):*	

Extend: Write about yourself in each of the perfect tenses. Past perfect: What did you do last summer? Present perfect: What are you learning in your classes? Future perfect: What would you like to do next summer? (These are only examples—feel free to choose your own subjects.)

© Houghton Mifflin Harcourt Publishing Company

 9.17A(i)
ELPS 4C, 5E

Review: Verbs 1

> **Underline** the verbs in the following sentences. Then identify auxiliary verbs with an **A** and linking verbs with an **L**.

1. My favorite meal <u>is</u> meatloaf and sweet potatoes. *(L above "is")*

2. Chris's younger brother and sister are twins.

3. Yolanda and Eric are always reading advice columns.

4. Grandpa has been forgetting where he puts his eyeglasses.

5. We were studying Emily Dickinson's poems last week.

6. My best friend and I attend the meetings for Young Diplomats.

7. Do you intend to run for re-election in the next presidential race?

8. Her motto is "Every day is an adventure."

9. Would you please wipe your shoes on the mat before coming in?

10. The sandwiches and salads were good.

11. Everyone was sorrowful when Mrs. Greene announced her retirement.

12. We used the Internet to find things to do during the summer vacation.

13. The choir gave a concert, and then they began their singing tour.

> **Write** a sentence using a present, past, or future tense verb.

_____

_____

> **Rewrite** your sentence using a perfect tense verb.

_____

_____

© Houghton Mifflin Harcourt Publishing Company

TEKS 9.17A(i)
ELPS 4C, 5E

Active & Passive Voice

A verb is said to be in the *active voice* when the subject is doing something. A verb is in the *passive voice* when the subject of the verb is being acted upon. Turn to 766.2 in *Write Source* for examples and more information.

> **Underline** the verbs in the following sentences. On the blank at the left, write whether the voice is active or passive. Some sentences contain more than one verb.

passive **1.** Lots of things <u>can be done</u> on the Internet.

_____ **2.** Most people send more e-mail than paper mail.

_____ **3.** Web sites include official government postings, information, and forms.

_____ **4.** Free on-line editions have been offered by many newspapers.

_____ **5.** Radio stations are playing music on the Internet.

_____ **6.** You can find a Web site for your favorite band, movie, or television show.

_____ **7.** Chess and other games are played across the Net by people who
_____ live on opposite sides of the world.

_____ **8.** Almost anything can be bought on the Net and delivered to
_____ your home.

_____ **9.** Certain Web sites allow you to control robots and other machines.

_____ **10.** Most companies have Web sites with information about their
_____ products, and some will send you free samples.

_____ **11.** In some areas, pizza can be ordered online.

_____ **12.** In the future, more and more people will go to school and college
via the Net.

Extend: Using an active voice, write three sentences about the Internet. Then rewrite them in the passive voice. Mark the sentences that you feel are strong and effective. Did you use active or passive voice in these sentences?

© Houghton Mifflin Harcourt Publishing Company

 ELPS 4C, 5E, 5G

Indicative & Imperative Moods

The mood of a verb indicates the tone or attitude with which a statement is made. The *indicative mood* is used to state a fact or to ask a question. The *imperative mood* is used to give a command. Turn to 768 in *Write Source*.

> **Write** *indicative* or *imperative* to indicate whether each underlined verb below is in the indicative or the imperative mood.

indicative **1.** Angela <u>intends</u> to continue her work at the animal shelter.

_____ **2.** Angela, <u>be</u> ready for difficult cases.

_____ **3.** Angela <u>expects</u> her joy of working with the animals to be both rewarding and challenging.

_____ **4.** Please <u>get</u> to work on time.

_____ **5.** The animals <u>love</u> Angela's attention.

_____ **6.** <u>Wait</u> your turn, Holly.

_____ **7.** Angela <u>lavishes</u> attention on each animal in her charge.

_____ **8.** Mr. Guzman, please <u>take</u> him home today.

_____ **9.** Can he <u>wait</u> until tomorrow?

_____ **10.** He <u>needs</u> a home today.

_____ **11.** Alright, you have <u>convinced</u> me.

_____ **12.** What do you <u>think</u> about your new home?

Extend: Think of a process that you understand well, such as how to prepare food, how to change a tire on a bicycle, or how to use a computer application. Write an instructional paragraph explaining how to perform the process. Use both the indicative and imperative moods in your instructions, but be sure to use the imperative mood when listing the specific steps in the process.

© Houghton Mifflin Harcourt Publishing Company

TEKS 9.17B
ELPS 4C, 5E

Subjunctive Mood

The mood of a verb indicates the tone or attitude with which a statement is made. The *subjunctive mood* is used to express a condition contrary to fact or highly doubtful, a wish, a possibility, a suggestion, or a necessity. Turn to 768 in *Write Source*.

Circle the sentence in each pair that is written in the subjunctive mood.

---

1. a. If I were you, I would apply for a scholarship.

   b. If you apply for several scholarships, you will likely get at least one of them.

2. a. Tiffany wishes she were spending her holiday break with friends.

   b. Tiffany may be able to spend her holiday break traveling with friends.

3. a. She looks forward to visiting several schools to explore many possibilities.

   b. Is it necessary that she visit so many schools to find just the right one?

4. a. Even though she is a good student, she wants to do better to get into the college of her dreams.

   b. If she were a better student, she would definitely get into the college of her dreams.

5. a. It is essential that she get her applications completed by the deadline.

   b. With the deadline looming, she feels the pressure to get her applications completed.

6. a. Tiffany has worked hard to become a better writer.

   b. Tiffany wishes she were a more clever writer.

Extend: Write three original sentences using the subjunctive mood. See page 768 of *Write Source*.

© Houghton Mifflin Harcourt Publishing Company

★ ELPS 4C, 5E, 5G

Transitive & Intransitive Verbs

A transitive verb shows action and is always followed by a direct object that receives the action. An intransitive verb refers to an action that is complete in itself. It does not need an object to receive the action. Turn to 760.1–760.2 in *Write Source*.

> **Underline** and label the verbs in the sentences below. Use *T* for transitive, *I* for intransitive. Circle all direct objects.

1. In 1925, Charles Francis Jenkins, an American, <u>envisioned</u> (television.) *T*

2. Vladimir Kosma Zworykin gave America its first camera tube, several years later.

3. Philo Farnsworth contributed greatly to the invention of television.

4. Three American scientists invented the transistor in 1947.

5. Inventors worked hard to overcome obstacles.

6. The first regularly scheduled black-and-white telecasts for the public began in 1939.

7. In 1941, the Federal Communications Commission (FCC) authorized public broadcasts in the United States.

8. By 1950, six million Americans owned television sets.

9. Color TV became available to most people in the 1960s.

10. The FCC authorized companies to broadcast color images in 1954.

11. Flat-screen televisions came on the scene in the 1980s.

12. Now digital signals create cleaner, sharper images than previous TV signals.

Extend: Write five sentences describing how your life would be different without television. Use both transitive and intransitive verbs. Exchange papers with a classmate. Underline all the verbs in each other's sentences. Indicate whether the verbs are transitive or intransitive and be prepared to explain why.

© Houghton Mifflin Harcourt Publishing Company

ELPS 4C, 5E

Direct & Indirect Objects

Direct objects and indirect objects receive the action of verbs and are usually nouns or pronouns. A sentence must have a direct object before it can have an indirect object. Turn to 760.2 in *Write Source*.

 Patty sang *Mother* a song.

Direct Object: song	**Indirect Object:** Mother
Who or *what* receives the action? (Patty sang *what?*)	*To whom* or *to what* was something done? (Patty sang *to whom?*)

> **Underline** and label the objects in the sentences below. Use *DO* for direct objects and *IO* for indirect objects. We've shown you how to use the question method.

                                                      DO

1. Ben Franklin witnessed man's first successful <u>flight</u>, which occurred in 1783 in

    a lighter-than-air balloon invented by the Montgolfier brothers.

       (Ask yourself, "Ben Franklin witnessed **what?**")

2. The lighter-than-air balloon prompted further experimentation with

    heavier-than-air gliders.

       (Ask yourself, "Balloon prompted **what?**")

3. Soon inventors were testing heavier-than-air flying machines.

4. The wings on these heavier-than-air gliders needed a special shape, one that

    would force air to flow much faster over the top than across the bottom.

5. Air pressure gives the wings the lift they need to carry heavy objects aloft.

       (Ask yourself, "Air pressure gives **what?**"

       (Ask yourself, "**To what** was something given?**")

6. The physical property of lift gave Orville and Wilbur Wright the opportunity to

    develop the first airplane.

       (Ask yourself, "The physical property of lift gave **what?**")

       (Ask yourself, "**To whom** was something given?**")

7. Past glider designs gave the Wright brothers a model for their self-propelled

    aircraft.

8. An evolution of imaginative experiments formed the modern airplane.

Extend: Write three to five sentences about your favorite activity. Use direct objects and indirect objects and label them *DO* or *IO* (as above).

© Houghton Mifflin Harcourt Publishing Company

 TEKS 9.17A(i)
ELPS 4C, 5E, 5G

Verbals: Gerunds, Infinitives, & Participles

Verbals (gerunds, infinitives, and participles) can strengthen your writing. Use them to clarify and describe your ideas. Turn to page 770 in *Write Source* for examples.

Types of Verbals	Noun	Adjective	Adverb
Gerund	X		
Infinitive	X	X	X
Participle		X	

Underline and label the verbals in the sentences below. Use *G* for gerunds, *I* for infinitives, and *P* for participles.

       G

1. Riding the roller coaster is the biggest thrill at the amusement park.

2. The first roller coaster to thrill Americans was built in 1884.

3. Built by popular demand, the roller coaster has become a familiar attraction; today you'll find about 2,000 of them in the United States alone.

4. Standing in line is part of the roller coaster experience.

5. All that waiting can be difficult!

6. Once secured safely in their cars, the riders have no escape.

7. To be hurtled straight into the air at more than 70 mph challenges the bravest passengers.

8. The clang of wheels on the rail builds tension in passengers anticipating the first dizzying drop.

9. Some people raise their hands to enhance the thrusting force of the ride.

10. Stay away from too much cotton candy to avoid roller-coaster sickness.

11. After the thrilling ride is over, why not get back in line?

12. Riding the roller coaster ends a perfect day at the amusement park.

Extend: Imagine riding a roller coaster or another amusement-park ride. In a paragraph, describe the sensations, using verbals to enhance your description. You might want to make a list of possible verbals. You could then create sentences using the verbals in your list.

© Houghton Mifflin Harcourt Publishing Company

⬤ ELPS 1C, 4C, 5E

Irregular Verbs 1

It's easy to form the past tense and past participle of regular verbs. You simply add *d* or *ed* to the present tense: *walk, walked,* (have) *walked.* Irregular verbs don't follow these simple rules: *begin, began,* (have) *begun.* You need to memorize the forms of irregular verbs. See the chart "Common Irregular Verbs and Their Principal Parts" at 764.2 in *Write Source.*

> **Write** the correct forms of the irregular verbs below. (The verbs appear in parentheses.)

1. Ernest Hemingway, one of the most influential writers of the early twentieth

   century, ____*is*____ admired by many writers today. *(am)*

2. In 1917 Hemingway _____ a career in journalism instead of attending

   college. *(choose)*

3. Hemingway's poor eyesight _____ him from joining the armed forces. *(keep)*

4. However, Hemingway _____ a volunteer ambulance driver in World

   War I. *(am)*

5. He _____ his famous novel The Sun Also Rises in 1926. *(write)*

6. This book _____ him fame. *(bring)*

7. Hemingway _____ to Europe and Africa, where he gathered material for his

   novels. *(go)*

8. After the United States entered World War II, Hemingway _____ German

   submarines in the Caribbean with an armed cabin cruiser. *(fight)*

9. In 1944, when the Germans _____, Hemingway followed as a war

   correspondent. *(flee)*

10. Hemingway was _____ the Pulitzer Prize for fiction in 1953, and he received

    the Nobel Prize for literature in 1954. *(give)*

Extend: Write sentences using the past tense and past participle of the following irregular verbs: *wear, know, do.*

© Houghton Mifflin Harcourt Publishing Company

★ ELPS 1C, 3C, 4C, 5E

Irregular Verbs 2

Regular verbs form their past and past participle by adding a *d* or an *ed* to the present tense: *talk, talked,* (have) *talked.* Irregular verbs form their past and past participle in some way other than the regular way: *sing, sang,* (have) *sung.* It is necessary to memorize the forms of irregular verbs. Turn to the list on page 764 in *Write Source.*

> **Circle** the correct verb forms in the sentences below.

1. Have you ((seen,) *see, saw*) the sunrise?

2. We often (*seen, see, saw*) the sunrise and hear the rooster crow.

3. I (*seen, see, saw*) the sunrise yesterday.

4. I have (*saw, seen*) the sunrise many times.

5. Mother asked me to (*sit, set*) the table.

6. I (*sit, sat*) and rested.

7. He (*throwed, threw, thrown*) the letter in the garbage.

8. Brighton will (*shake, shook, shaken, shakes*) with fear during storms.

9. Our dog (*shaked, shook, shaken, shakes*) with fear during the storm last night.

10. Bridget and Cleo have (*weave, wove, woven*) rugs for the craft fair next Friday.

11. The kindergarten class (*draw, drew, drawn*) pictures yesterday.

12. All the fruit salad has been (*eat, ate, eaten*).

13. The full moon (*shine, shone, shined*) on the lake as Margaret (*shined, shone*) her

    new shoes.

14. Have you (*drunken, drank, drunk*) the lake water?

15. We (*fleed, fled*) before the water rose.

16. Both of them (*come, came*) whenever I call.

17. Both of them (*come, came*) whenever I called.

Extend: Correct all your errors in the sentences above. Read the corrected sentences aloud several times. In this way, you train your ear to hear the correct usage.

© Houghton Mifflin Harcourt Publishing Company

Irregular Verbs 3

The principal parts of irregular verbs don't fit a simple pattern, so you need to memorize them. See 764.2 in *Write Source* for a list of some irregular verbs and their parts.

> **Correct** the mistakes below by writing the proper verb above the underlined words.

1. Tornadoes, also known as twisters or cyclones, have *took* many lives. *(taken)*

2. Tornadoes have <u>tore</u> towns apart and left paths of destruction 50 miles wide.

3. A tornado creates extreme low pressure that can cause buildings to explode as the tornado's effect is <u>feel</u>.

4. Tornadoes can <u>dragged</u> objects for miles.

5. When a tornado warning is issued, people <u>went</u> to basements for safety.

6. A tornado <u>hanged</u> in the air.

7. Later the huge funnel <u>sinked</u> to the ground, and we <u>run</u> to the basement.

8. One shocked man just <u>sitted</u> and watched the funnel cloud approach.

9. Another man <u>lied</u> in a ditch, covering his head.

10. Dad watched as the tornado <u>dived</u> toward the ground.

11. After the tornado, it was clear that many trees had <u>fell</u>.

12. The neighbor's fence had been <u>threw</u> down the street.

13. The tornado had <u>blew</u> away one building, while leaving another building a few feet away untouched.

14. People <u>come</u> from far away to help the victims of the tornado.

15. A tornado's tremendous destruction has often <u>gave</u> many people a feeling of despair.

Extend: Write three sentences for each verb you used incorrectly in the above sentences.

© Houghton Mifflin Harcourt Publishing Company

⭐ **ELPS** 1C, 3C, 4C

Irregular Verbs: *Lie* and *Lay*

Here are the principal parts of *lie* and *lay*.

Present	Present Participle	Past	Past Participle
Lie *(to recline)* **I want to *lie* down.**	**(am) lying**	**lay**	**(have) lain**
Lay *(to put down)* **I *lay* my books on the table.**	**(am) laying**	**laid**	**(have) laid**

> **Circle** the correct word in the parentheses in each of the sentences below.

1. The little baby (*lay,* *lie*) quietly in the corner of his crib.

2. After their 50-mile march, the soldiers (*lay, laid*) in their tents.

3. Where is my pen? I know I (*laid, lay*) it down here yesterday.

4. They have (*laid, lain*) the blankets on the ground in preparation for the concert.

5. She was (*laying, lying*) clothes out on the bed.

6. Last night I (*laid, lay*) awake in bed, listening to the storm.

7. I (*laid, lay*) my head upon the pillow.

8. If you are tired, (*lay, lie*) down on the sofa.

9. I was so exhausted that I could have (*lain, laid*) in bed all day.

10. Our hens are (*laying, lying*) eggs.

11. Please, (*lie, lay*) the newspaper down and talk to me.

12. Have you (*lain, laid*) the tile in the bath?

13. I'm going home and (*lay, lie*) in the sun.

14. That tree has been (*laying, lying*) in the lake since the storm.

15. Grandma has been (*laying, lying*) on the couch.

16. Does that rug (*lie, lay*) smoothly?

Extend: If you have trouble using *lie* and *lay,* read the sentences above aloud (after you are certain you have chosen the correct form). Read them several times. Hearing the correct form of *lie* and *lay* helps you learn them.

© Houghton Mifflin Harcourt Publishing Company

Review: Verbs 2

> **Underline** and label the verbs in the sentences below. (In sentences with more than a one-word verb, be sure to underline the whole verb phrase.) Write *A* above a phrase containing an auxiliary verb and *L* above a linking verb.

1. Francine was helping her grandma.

2. The American eagle appears on the endangered-species list.

3. Oksana will reach the top of the mountain in less than a week.

4. The bear is badly injured.

5. At breakfast, the milk smelled spoiled.

6. I am telling you for the last time.

> **Underline** the verbs below. Write *T* above a transitive verb and *I* above an intransitive verb. If the verb is transitive, write *DO* above the direct object and *IO* above any indirect object.

1. Justin covered his book with aluminum foil.

2. The eagle flew across the river.

3. Why don't you give Peter the assignment at the end of class?

4. Peter strutted down the street.

5. Chia baked me a loaf of banana nut bread.

6. I threw my dog the ball.

> **Underline** and label the verbals in the following sentences. Use *G* for gerund, *I* for infinitive, or *P* for participle.

1. Running is good exercise.

2. I really like to run on a treadmill.

3. The quarterback, faking a pass, ran in for the touchdown.

© Houghton Mifflin Harcourt Publishing Company

ELPS 4C

4. I know you are going to track mud all over the house if I let you in.

5. I enjoy tracking.

6. The hunter tracking the deer stopped to catch his breath.

Write the correct forms of the verbs (in parentheses) in the blanks in the sentences below.

1. He shouldn't have _____ down there. *(lie)*

2. I _____ the turkey sandwich yesterday. *(eat)*

3. The company had _____ him a letter. *(write)*

4. Last week the athlete _____ the channel in about an hour. *(swim)*

5. Pat had _____ his shirt while working on the car. *(tear)*

6. The magician _____ me her sleeve before she performed the trick. *(show)*

7. The game was canceled because it had _____ to rain. *(begin)*

8. The man _____ the stray dog to the animal shelter. *(take)*

Fill in the missing principal parts for the following irregular verbs.

	Present Tense	Past Tense	Past Participle
1.	go	_____	_____
2.	wear	_____	_____
3.	_____	kept	_____
4.	_____	_____	sung
5.	speak	_____	_____
6.	_____	_____	taken
7.	_____	_____	shown
8.	_____	swung	_____
9.	_____	did	_____

© Houghton Mifflin Harcourt Publishing Company

ELPS 4C

Pretest: Adjectives & Adverbs

> **Underline** the adjectives (except for any articles: *a*, *an*, or *the*) and draw arrows to the nouns they modify. Circle each adverb and draw an arrow to the verb, adjective, or adverb that it modifies.

1. Theodore Roosevelt advised, "Walk softly, but carry a big stick."

2. The singer filled the immense hall with a magnificent voice.

3. Pumpkins and corn grow well in the Midwest.

4. Harsh winters in the Alaskan wilderness claimed many lives during the Gold Rush.

5. It certainly appears that the tournament is running smoothly.

6. Obi-Wan Kenobi said quietly, "May the Force be with you."

7. The Italian restaurant sold more deep-dish pizzas this year than last year.

8. The turbo-charged car swerved dangerously around the corner.

> **Write** out the positive, the comparative, and/or the superlative forms of the following adjectives and adverbs.

	Positive	Comparative	Superlative
1.	*fantastic*	*more fantastic*	most fantastic
2.		taller	
3.	closely		
4.	hungry		
5.			worst
6.		prettier	
7.			most likely
8.			soonest

© Houghton Mifflin Harcourt Publishing Company

Adjectives

An adjective describes or in some way modifies a noun or pronoun. The articles—*a, an, the*—are always considered adjectives. Turn to page 772 in *Write Source*.

> **Insert** an appropriate adjective on each blank below. Use interesting and powerful adjectives to make the information come alive. Try not to repeat adjectives.

1   A couple of years ago, I started working at the high school radio station.

2   It's a ___*wonderful*___ experience. I help out by teaching _____ students

3   and disc jockeys how to be _____ speakers. On the radio, it isn't

4   _____ to talk in __ _____ voice. A DJ has to be _____

5   and _____ . Only by having ___ _____ voice does the DJ keep

6   _____ listeners from tuning out between _____ _____ hits.

7   Many people scoff at the idea that the DJ matters, but don't you have ___

8   _____ DJ on the station you listen to? The question is, "What makes him

9   or her so _____ ?" Is she very _____? Is he unusually _____ ?

10 I give examples of _____ speaking voices. I know that each person will

11 have his or her own _____ style, but my _____ pointers help

12 the student DJ's see the effect of their styles. I would much rather listen to a

13 DJ who is _____ than one who seems _____ or _____ .

14 The next time you listen to your radio, see if you can pick out the

15 _____ DJ's from _____ _____ ones.

Extend: Choose an author you enjoy and select a passage from one of her or his books. Make a list of the adjectives you find there. Share your list with a classmate. Ask questions such as "How often does this author use adjectives?"; "Which adjectives are the most powerful?"; or "How do the adjectives add to the passage?" To help answer these questions, read each sentence aloud, leaving out all the adjectives.

© Houghton Mifflin Harcourt Publishing Company

ELPS 4C, 5E

Predicate Adjectives

Any adjective that follows a form of the verb "be" (or other linking verb) and describes the subject is a predicate adjective. Turn to 772.1 in *Write Source*.

> **Put** parentheses around the sentence in each pair that does not contain a predicate adjective. In the other sentence, underline the simple subject once and underline a predicate adjective twice.

1. a. (Ever since the fifth grade, I have played the saxophone in the school band.)

   b. Band <u>class</u> seemed <u>challenging</u> then, but I met a real challenge in high school.

2. a. Marching band replaced band class as the hardest thing I'd ever done.

   b. It may look easy, but marching while playing an instrument is very difficult.

3. a. Not only did I (and everyone else in the band) have to memorize the music, but we also had to remember how we had to move on the field.

   b. That was hard to do, especially when we practiced the music only a few times in the band room before starting to learn the marching maneuvers.

4. a. I know some people think marching bands are silly.

   b. I travel with a great group of friends, visiting places I wouldn't see on my own.

5. a. Last year we traveled to Boston for a parade that honored war veterans.

   b. Our band felt honored when the Rolling Along Veteran Band, all in wheelchairs, asked us to play a concert with them.

6. a. We sound great at sporting events, and we look good in our uniforms.

   b. Everyone's friends and family come to watch us and cheer us on.

Extend: Write three to five sentences about playing in a band (based on your experience or your imagination). Use linking verbs with predicate adjectives in your sentences. Then try to think of some action verbs to use in place of the linking verb + predicate adjective combination. Which version do you prefer?

© Houghton Mifflin Harcourt Publishing Company

ELPS 4C, 5E

Forms of Adjectives

Adjectives take three forms: *positive* (describing a noun or pronoun without comparing it to anything), *comparative* (comparing two nouns), and *superlative* (comparing three or more persons, places, things, or ideas). Turn to 772.2 in *Write Source*.

> **Read** each sentence below. Then rewrite it using the positive, comparative, and/or superlative form of the underlined adjective.

1. *Positive:* Michael Jordan was a good basketball player.

2. *Comparative:* Michael Jordan was a better basketball player than Larry Bird.

3. *Superlative:* _____

4. *Positive:* _____

5. *Comparative:* Dracula is a scarier creature than Godzilla.

6. *Superlative:* _____

7. *Positive:* _____

8. *Comparative:* _____

9. *Superlative:* That was the best meal I've ever eaten.

10. *Positive:* I feel silly today.

11. *Comparative:* _____

12. *Superlative:* _____

13. *Positive:* _____

14. *Comparative:* _____

15. *Superlative:* This is the most remarkable painting I've seen all day.

Extend: Compose three to five sentences containing positive adjectives. Next rewrite each sentence using the comparative and superlative forms. Would one of your sentences be an excellent beginning statement for a piece of writing?

© Houghton Mifflin Harcourt Publishing Company

ELPS 4C

Review: Adjectives

> **Underline** all the adjectives in the sentences below. Write *C* above a comparative adjective, *S* above a superlative adjective, and *P* above all predicate adjectives.

1. That dog is exceptionally friendly.

2. A family dog should be both well-trained and cooperative.

3. I think golden retrievers are better than greyhounds as family dogs.

4. Labrador retrievers are also good pets, especially for children.

5. If you like gentle, intelligent dogs, then nothing can compare to the collie.

6. Poodles can be large or small and are frequently crossbred with other dogs.

7. A graceful, quick dog, the Siberian husky is also alert and strong.

8. Loyal, gentle, and intelligent sheepdogs herd and guard sheep.

9. The Chinese shar-pei has loose skin, many wrinkles, and a blue-black tongue.

10. Every dog needs nutritious food and fresh water every day.

11. Most dogs are energetic and enjoy walking, running, and playing.

12. Dogs require more care than cats.

13. Some dogs are intelligent; others are strong.

14. Many people think the smallest dog is the Chihuahua.

15. Most dogs are loyal companions, and they need owners who are equally faithful.

16. Perhaps the biggest challenge for busy owners is spending time with their dog.

17. You can often find a suitable dog at an animal shelter.

18. Having a dog is hard work, but it can be very enjoyable.

© Houghton Mifflin Harcourt Publishing Company

ELPS 4C

Adverbs

Adverbs modify a verb, an adjective, or another adverb. They tell the reader *how, when, where, why, how often,* or *how much* something happens. This exercise will help you identify adverbs. Turn to page 774 in *Write Source.*

> **Underline** the adverbs in the following sentences. The correct number of adverbs in each sentence is given in parentheses.

1. My parents <u>regularly</u> invite friends over for dinner. (*1*)

2. I rarely help prepare for the dinners, but I badly needed to make some money and I knew my parents would really appreciate the help. (*3*)

3. My mother left me a list of "things to do," and I very diligently worked my way through it. (*2*)

4. I precisely measured and carefully chopped the ingredients for the meal. (*2*)

5. I had almost everything ready when the phone suddenly rang. (*1*)

6. I quickly jumped up to answer it and accidentally knocked the cutting board and three full bowls of ingredients to the floor. (*3*)

7. I stood completely stunned for a moment and then answered the phone. (*2*)

8. My mother cheerily said she'd called to see how I was doing and that she'd return shortly. (*2*)

9. I reluctantly said okay, slowly hung up the phone, and dejectedly looked at the mess covering the floor. (*3*)

10. I sulked for a moment, then busily cleaned up the mass of ingredients that covered the floor. (*2*)

11. We had enough extra ingredients in the house for me to hurriedly duplicate all my work . . . without my mother ever knowing what had happened. (*2*)

Extend: List the adverbs in the above exercise on a piece of your own paper. Catalog each adverb by time, place, manner, or degree. See 774.

© Houghton Mifflin Harcourt Publishing Company

ELPS 4C, 5E

Types of Adverbs

An adverb modifies a verb, an adjective, or another adverb. Adverbs can be cataloged in four basic ways: time, place, manner, and degree. Turn to 774.1 in *Write Source*.

> **Rewrite** the sentences below following the instructions in parentheses. In the blank at the left, tell whether the italicized adverb shows time, place, manner, or degree.

degree   **1.** Growing up on a cattle ranch proved to be a memorable experience for me. (Add *highly* and use it to modify an adjective.)

    Growing up on a cattle ranch proved to be a highly memorable

    experience for me.

_____ **2.** Dad would have liked many boys to help him, but he and Mom had eight girls before they had a boy. (Add *finally* to modify a verb.)

_____ **3.** Dad told the other ranchers, "Girls are as good as boys." (Add *unexpectedly* to modify an action verb.)

_____ **4.** While other ranchers rolled their eyes, Dad rolled up his sleeves to help us prove his statement. (Add *backward* to modify a verb.)

_____ **5.** We painstakingly learned to drive trucks and operate combines. (Add *very* to modify an adverb.)

Extend: Use the five italicized adverbs in parentheses above in sentences of your own. Circle each adverb and draw an arrow to the verb, adjective, or adverb it modifies.

© Houghton Mifflin Harcourt Publishing Company

ELPS 4C

Forms of Adverbs

Adverbs, like adjectives, have three forms: *positive, comparative,* and *superlative.* (Turn to 774.2 in *Write Source.*) Use the comparative form to compare two things, the superlative to compare three or more. Most one-syllable adverbs take the endings *-er* or *-est* (*soon, sooner, soonest*) to create the comparative and superlative forms; but longer adverbs and almost all those ending in *-ly* use *more* and *most* or *less* and *least* (*more ambitiously, most ambitiously; less ambitiously, least ambitiously*).

> **Add** an adverb to each sentence below. Be sure to use the correct form.

1. The part of growing up on a ranch that I liked ____*best*____ of all was having

   acres and acres of native prairie to roam.

2. One part of ranching that I did very _____ was riding horses.

3. The horses moved quite _____.

4. Whenever my horse veered suddenly to put a cow back in the herd, I had to try

   _____ to stay in the saddle.

5. Susan, my sister, was a great rider, and she could control horses _____

   than I could.

6. For pleasure riding, we used several horses, and I liked Goldie _____ of

   all because she was a Tennessee Walker with a smooth gait.

7. We went on trail rides _____ than most children.

8. Dad would _____ carry us in a blanket.

9. On an early summer morn, my sister and I often rode _____ to the top

   of Juneberry Hill to pick berries.

10. Mom, compared to all the rest of us, was the _____ likely to drive our

    pickup.

11. She packed picnic breakfasts _____ than I did.

12. After eating, we would _____ fill our buckets with berries and head for

    home.

© Houghton Mifflin Harcourt Publishing Company

ELPS 2I, 3E–3G, 4C, 5E

Using *Good* and *Well*

Good is always used as an adjective. *Well* can be used as either an adjective or an adverb. Turn to page 734 in *Write Source*.

> **I get *good* grades.** (*Good* is an adjective; it modifies the noun *grades*.)

> **I am *good*.** (*Good* is a predicate adjective that describes *I*. *Good* is used as an adjective to mean "able" or "not bad.")

> **I am *well*.** (*Well* is a predicate adjective that describes *I*. *Well* is used as an adjective to mean "healthy.")

> **He sang *well*.** (*Well* is an adverb; it modifies *sang*.)

Circle the correct word (*good* or *well*) in the following sentences. Draw an arrow to the word that *good* or *well* modifies.

1. The circus had a number of very (good, well) acts.

2. The trained seals performed exceptionally (good, well)!

3. It must take a long time to train seals that (good, well).

4. The ringmaster introduced the acts (good, well).

5. It is (good, well) that the lions are well-trained.

6. The lion tamer seems to know each lion (good, well).

7. The flying trapeze acts went (good, well).

8. Every band member plays several instruments (good, well).

9. Laughing at the clowns felt (good, well).

10. The hot dogs always taste so (good, well) at a circus.

11. It was (good, well) that we took our little sisters and brothers with us.

12. They behaved surprisingly (good, well).

13. It must take a lot of practice to be a (good, well) clown.

14. Roasted peanuts smell (good, well).

15. Going to the circus makes everyone feel (good, well).

Extend: Write three to five sentences using *good* and *well*. Exchange papers with a classmate and discuss whether you have used these words correctly.

© Houghton Mifflin Harcourt Publishing Company

Review: Adverbs

> Circle all the adverbs in the following narrative. There are 40 adverbs.

1   It was (so) hot! We sweated as we marched slowly under the scorching sun.

2   Our wool band uniforms grew heavier and heavier, clinging more and more

3   tightly to our bodies. Suddenly, the tuba player fell backward. Several

4   paramedics rushed to him and quickly moved him to the sideline. Still we

5   marched on, regally and precisely.

6   Then, a flute player fell down. The front three rows marched away

7   because they had not seen the girl faint. The rest of the band stopped,

8   however. Watching the chaos, the band director blew his whistle sharply. Now

9   the front rows stopped abruptly—a half-dozen paces away. Several parents

10   began vigorously fanning the flute player. The band director told us to take off

11   our jackets and hats. (We laid them neatly on the curb.) Firefighters and

12   paramedics began passing cups of water around. Finally, the flute player

13   revived, and someone carefully helped her to the curb.

14   When the mayhem was over, the band director blew his whistle twice, and

15   we quickly re-formed. We had just marched past the reviewing stand when

16   suddenly water was swirling everywhere! The firefighters had opened a

17   hydrant. Spectators, both young and old, began to splash one another with

18   water. Some people sat down in the cool spray. We stood frozen in our rows,

19   waiting for a whistle blast that would tell us what to do next. The band

20   director just stood silently, staring blankly. Apparently he had never

21   encountered anything like this. "Go back to the gym," he said. "Quickly get

22   into your street clothes, and let's get cool."

© Houghton Mifflin Harcourt Publishing Company

ELPS 4C

Pretest: Prepositions, Conjunctions, & Interjections

> **Underline** the prepositional phrases in the following sentences. Then circle each preposition and write *O* above each object of the preposition.

1. Step (behind) the line so that you can shoot the free throw.

2. Yikes! What is in the attic?

3. Since you seem to have so many of the answers, you do it.

4. Though she had polio as a child, Wilma Rudolph won gold medals during the 1960 Olympic Games in Rome.

5. Organ donors give the gift of life, yet many people do not have the donor sticker placed on their drivers' licenses.

6. Good grief! Both the emu and the ostrich are born with weird legs.

7. Throughout history, people have studied the stars and the planets.

8. Either pull the weeds out of the flower bed or shovel the grain into the grainery.

9. If you look out the bus window and peer down the street, you can see the tower on top of the John Hancock Building.

> **List** the interjections and conjunctions from the sentences above, placing each in the appropriate column below.

Interjections	Coordinating Conjunctions	Subordinating Conjunctions	Correlative Conjunctions

© Houghton Mifflin Harcourt Publishing Company

★ ELPS 3E, 4C

Prepositions & Interjections

A preposition is a word (or group of words) that shows the relationship between its object (a noun or a pronoun that follows the preposition) and another word in the sentence. Turn to page 776 in *Write Source*.

An interjection is included in a sentence in order to communicate emotion or surprise. Interjections are set off from the rest of the sentence with either a comma or an exclamation point. Turn to page 778 in *Write Source*.

> **Underline** the prepositional phrases in the following narrative and then circle the prepositions. Write *INT* above any interjections.

1   *INT*
    "Hey, Rita!" Bill called as he saw Rita limping (toward) him (on) crutches.

2   "Why are you wearing a cast? What happened to you?"

3   "Hi, Bill," Rita said as she looked up at him. "I guess you didn't hear that I

4   was in a car accident last week."

5   "Wow! No, I didn't hear. I'm sorry. Was anyone else in the car with you?"

6   "Yeah, my little brother," she said.

7   "I hope he wasn't hurt! I can't imagine the amount of trouble I'd get in if

8   my little brother got hurt while I was driving," Bill said.

9   "No kidding! My brother was actually thrown out of the car when the

10 passenger door popped open. He landed about 15 feet from the car in an

11 overgrown ditch. But he wasn't hurt, except for a few scrapes."

12 "Whew! Thank goodness for that," said Bill.

13 "I'd just gotten done telling him to wear his seat belt," Rita said. "Mom

14 really yelled at him when she found out he hadn't been wearing it." Rita

15 leaned back against the wall and moved her crutches so she could lean on

16 them.

Extend I: Copy a passage from a book or write down lyrics to a song and then underline all the prepositional phrases. In a small group, compare your work. Were prepositional phrases used a lot?

Extend II: Try to go an entire day without using any interjections. Or, write down every interjection you use in a day.

© Houghton Mifflin Harcourt Publishing Company

ELPS 4C, 5B

Coordinating Conjunctions

Words, phrases, and clauses are often connected to one another by coordinating conjunctions such as *and, but, or, for, nor, so,* and *yet.* Coordinating conjunctions link words, phrases, or clauses that are equal or of the same type. Turn to page 778. Study the chart "Kinds of Conjunctions."

> **Underline** all of the coordinating conjunctions in the following passage.

1   I've been playing soccer a long time, <u>so</u> it seems like second nature to me.

2   I started when I was only eight and have played every year since then. At first

3   my parents were worried that I might get hurt, but when they saw me play,

4   they were impressed and encouraged me to continue. I have never been injured

5   while playing, nor have I ever missed a game. (Actually, I did miss one game

6   for a family vacation, but I told my coaches ahead of time.)

7   I think it's odd that soccer is so popular in other countries, yet in the

8   United States it's one of the least popular team sports. I realize that it has

9   become more popular over the past few years, but I think soccer is much more

10   fun and interesting than baseball, football, or hockey. Some people say it's a

11   boring sport and has no strategy to it, but I think those people aren't truly

12   familiar with the game.

13   Soccer is all about strategy, but it's not the slow, plodding strategy of

14   football. Soccer demands a fast-paced, think-on-your-feet strategy: *Where's the*

15   *ball? Who's most likely to get the next pass? Can I intercept or should I pull*

16   *back and defend? What is the main weakness or bad habit of the opposing*

17   *goalie?* All of these questions race through my mind as I'm playing, and I have

18   to decide what's best for the team and which options will ultimately pay off in

19   the form of a goal.

Extend: Write a paragraph explaining how you can use coordinating conjunctions in sentences to improve your writing. Include examples to illustrate your point. You might begin, "I often use coordinating conjunctions to join two sentences."

© Houghton Mifflin Harcourt Publishing Company

 TEKS 9.13C
ELPS 4C, 5E, 5F

Correlative Conjunctions

Correlative conjunctions are conjunctions used in pairs. Turn to 778.2 in *Write Source* for examples and more information. Also use the chart "Kinds of Conjunctions" on page 778.

> **Write** sentences using the correlative conjunctions that are listed in the parentheses.

1. *(not only, but also)*

I not only like oatmeal for breakfast, but I also like it for lunch.

2. *(both, and)*

_____

_____

3. *(either, or)*

_____

_____

4. *(neither, nor)*

_____

_____

5. *(whether, or)*

_____

_____

6. *(both, and)*

_____

_____

7. *(not only, but also)*

_____

_____

Extend: Edit a piece of your writing. Try to join short sentences with correlative conjunctions to make longer, stronger statements.

© Houghton Mifflin Harcourt Publishing Company

 **ELPS** 2I, 3C, 4C, 5E, 5F

Subordinating Conjunctions

A subordinating conjunction connects a dependent clause to an independent clause. Turn to 778.3 in *Write Source*. Also use the chart "Kinds of Conjunctions."

> **Join** the following sentence pairs using a subordinating conjunction. Consider which sentence should become the subordinate clause, and whether it should begin or end the sentence.

1. My mother gave me guitar lessons for a gift. It was my birthday.

Since it was my birthday, my mother gave me guitar lessons for a gift.

_____

2. I could take them any time I wanted. I began my first lesson in the summer.

_____

_____

3. I went to the music store. My teacher showed me different kinds of guitars.

_____

_____

4. He showed me the six different strings on the guitar. He explained the guitar's other parts.

_____

_____

5. My first lesson went well. My mother took me to get some frozen yogurt.

_____

_____

6. I practice an hour every day. I want to join a band.

_____

_____

Extend: Write five to eight sentences, each containing a different subordinating conjunction. Read your sentences to a classmate and ask him or her to identify each subordinating conjunction.

© Houghton Mifflin Harcourt Publishing Company

Review: Prepositions, Conjunctions, & Interjections

Underline each interjection once and each preposition twice in the sentences below. Then circle each conjunction and identify it by writing coordinating, correlative, or subordinating on the blank at the left.

coordinating   **1.** <u>Yeah</u>, I have the ball (and) the bat <u>in</u> my basement.

_____ **2.** <u>Hey!</u> Where do you think you're going with my bat and ball?

_____ **3.** In spite of all the time I've spent on the shores of Lake Michigan, I have learned neither how to swim nor how to sail.

_____ **4.** After we went to the basketball game, I wanted a basketball hoop in my backyard.

_____ **5.** Yipes, that bee nearly stung you while you weren't looking.

_____ **6.** I think we can see both the Badlands and Yellowstone National Park during our two-week vacation.

_____ **7.** No! I will not eat mashed potatoes with gravy after the gravy gets cold.

_____ **8.** I'll go to the store while you're gone.

_____ **9.** Oh, well! Jevon will have to go home before the game is over if he doesn't want to get into trouble.

_____ **10.** I went down the hole, through the tunnel, and into the water to finally retrieve my hat.

_____ **11.** My gosh, you have grown since I last saw you.

_____ **12.** Yes, my brother threw three touchdown passes, but we still lost the game.

_____ **13.** I don't want to hear about any problems the babysitter had with you while I was gone.

_____ **14.** Ouch! I burnt my tongue when I tasted the pizza..

_____ **15.** The Pony Express riders made their deliveries whether it snowed or not.

© Houghton Mifflin Harcourt Publishing Company

ELPS 4C

Review: Parts of Speech Activities

Identify the part of speech that each underlined word represents. Use the following labels: *N* for noun, *V* for verb, *PRO* for pronoun, *ADJ* for adjective, *ADV* for adverb, *PREP* for preposition, *C* for conjunction, and *I* for interjection.

$\qquad\qquad\qquad\qquad\qquad\qquad\qquad$ ADJ

1 This summer I'm going on a <u>backpacking</u> trip with my friend Aaron

2 <u>and</u> his <u>dad</u>. We're going to hike <u>through</u> Yellowstone National Park for

3 five days. Backpacking is a lot <u>like</u> camping, <u>but</u> you have to carry

4 everything <u>you</u> need while you hike.

5 Aaron <u>has been</u> backpacking <u>before</u>, <u>so</u> last weekend he <u>helped</u> me load my

6 new backpack so I could practice using it. The first thing <u>we</u> packed was

7 clothing, including a <u>warm</u> sweater and jeans for when we go up into the

8 <u>mountains</u>—it gets cold <u>there</u>! Next I added a <u>small</u> bag <u>with</u> my flashlight,

9 my toothbrush, and some sunscreen. Then I <u>attached</u> my sleeping bag to the

10 bottom <u>of</u> the pack.

11 I <u>will have</u> to carry more than just my personal <u>gear</u>, though. <u>Our</u> camp

12 stove <u>and</u> a big cooking pot went <u>into</u> my pack next. They're <u>really</u> heavy, <u>but</u>

13 <u>Aaron</u> has to carry something even heavier: our tent.

14 <u>Though</u> I don't think I'll be able to make it for long, Aaron <u>says</u> that I'll be

15 walking around <u>easily</u> once I get used to the pack on my shoulders. He says

16 the trails are <u>not</u> exactly like sidewalks in our neighborhood. In fact, <u>some</u>

17 may be <u>snow-covered</u>, rocky, and steep. <u>When</u> we go up into the mountains,

18 we will have to adjust to the <u>higher</u> elevations. <u>Wow</u>, I can't wait.

© Houghton Mifflin Harcourt Publishing Company

ELPS 4C

Complete the following statements.

1. A _____*noun*_____ is a word that names a person, a place, a thing, or an idea.

2. When a noun or a pronoun is used as a direct object, an _____, or

an _____, it is in the objective case.

3. When a noun or a pronoun shows ownership, it is in the _____ case.

4. A _____ can be used in place of a noun.

5. A _____ or a _____ is used as the subject of a sentence or a clause.

6. *Who, whose, whom, which,* and *that* are _____ .

7. A _____ expresses action or a state of being.

8. *I see* is an example of the _____ tense; *I saw* is an example of the

_____ tense; *I will see* is an example of the _____ tense.

9. In the following sentence, the word _____ is the direct object:

The boy proudly showed me his skateboard.

10. In the following sentence, the word _____ is an indirect

object: *Ruth-Anne gave me an extravagant birthday present.*

11. Adjectives describe or modify _____ or _____ .

12. Adverbs modify _____ , _____ , or _____ .

13. The word *smart* is a predicate _____ in the following sentence:

Tarzan is smart.

14. In the phrase *behind the door,* the word *behind* is a _____ .

15. The words *and, but, or, nor, for, yet,* and *so* are coordinating _____ .

16. A _____ connects individual words or groups of words.

17. An _____ shows strong emotion or surprise.

© Houghton Mifflin Harcourt Publishing Company

Sentence Activities

The activities in this section cover three important areas: (1) the basic parts, types, and kinds of sentences as well as agreement issues; (2) methods for writing smooth-reading sentences; and (3) common sentence errors. Most activities include practice in which you review, combine, or analyze different sentences. In addition, the **Extend** activities will give follow-up practice with certain skills.

Sentence Basics **127**

Sentence Combining **157**

Sentence Problems **163**

Sentence Review **187**

© Houghton Mifflin Harcourt Publishing Company

ELPS 4C

Pretest: Subjects & Predicates

> **Underline** the simple subject once and the simple predicate twice in the following sentences. If the subject is understood, as in the first statement, insert the understood subject within parentheses.

(You)
1. Bring the chair over here, please.

2. The cat ate the tuna-fish sandwich.

3. What is keeping them?

4. They are playing soccer on field number four.

5. You can help your dad with the laundry.

6. Where is Jacqui's blue-sequined dress?

7. Thomas Alva Edison invented the phonograph and the electric lightbulb.

8. Put more slack on the sail!

> **Underline** the complete subject once and the complete predicate twice in the following sentences. If either the subject or predicate is compound, write **C** above it.

C
1. Red, yellow, and orange tulips grow and flourish in Holland.

2. From small, plain caterpillars come bright and beautiful butterflies.

3. Hamburgers, hot dogs, and tacos are my favorite foods.

4. Fly-fishing and canoeing are popular activities in Wisconsin and Minnesota.

5. Students should walk quickly to the exits if the alarm sounds.

6. Are you and Rosa walking or riding your bikes to the park?

7. Evel Knievel jumped motorcycles over cars, buses, walls, and even buildings.

8. Elk, moose, and other large mammals inhabit Yellowstone National Park.

9. Ginger Rogers and Fred Astaire tap-danced and tangoed their way through many old films during the '30s and '40s.

© Houghton Mifflin Harcourt Publishing Company

 **TEKS** 9.13C, 9.17C
ELPS 4C, 5E, 5G

Simple Subjects & Predicates

All sentences must have a subject (noun or pronoun) and a predicate (verb) and express a complete thought. A simple subject is the subject without the words that modify it. A simple predicate is the verb without the words that modify it. Turn to 780.1 and 782.1 in *Write Source* for examples.

> **Underline** the simple subjects once and the simple predicates twice in the following sentences.

1. Many <u>aspects</u> of daily life <u>depend</u> upon electricity.

2. Electricity is a basic part of the matter in the universe.

3. In the human body, electrical signals carry information to and from the brain.

4. Electrical signals tell the brain what the eyes see, what the ears hear, and what the fingers feel.

5. The brain, using electrical signals, tells muscles to move.

6. During the 1800s, people learned to use electricity to do work.

7. Soon inventors learned to generate electrical energy in large quantities.

8. Electricity has many practical applications.

9. Lighting, one practical application, has changed the way people live.

10. Could you imagine life without electricity?

11. Computers use electricity to process information.

12. Without electricity, modern manufacturing would be impossible.

13. Satellites use electrical energy to send information around the world.

14. Most cars depend on an electric spark to start the engine.

15. Yes, electricity makes our lives more productive.

Extend: Write a paragraph describing what your life would be like without electricity. Underline each simple subject once and each simple predicate twice. Look carefully at your subjects and predicates. Could you use a more specific noun for some subjects or a stronger verb for some predicates?

© Houghton Mifflin Harcourt Publishing Company

TEKS 9.17C
ELPS 4C

Simple, Complete, & Compound Subjects and Predicates

A simple subject or predicate is the subject or predicate without the words that describe or modify it. The complete subject or predicate includes the simple subject or predicate and all the words that modify or explain it. Compound subjects or predicates are composed of two or more simple subjects or predicates. Turn to 780.1 and 782.1 in *Write Source* for examples.

> **Circle** the simple subjects and underline the simple predicates in the following sentences. Draw a line between the complete subject and the complete predicate. Write **CS** above compound subjects and **CP** above compound predicates.

1. Scientists conduct research in Antarctica.

2. Antarctica—the world's coldest, windiest, highest continent—is not an easy place to work.

3. Harsh conditions face the men and women who go there.

4. The world's biggest laboratory, Antarctica is reserved for science by international agreement.

5. Scientists recorded the world's lowest temperature there: −89.2° C (−128.6° F).

6. Antarctic winds average 44 miles per hour, but they can gust to 120 miles per hour.

7. Most scientists and support staff conduct research from spring through fall and head home for the winter (which is actually summer in the Northern Hemisphere).

8. Complete darkness and extreme cold isolate Antarctica and discourage research during the six-month-long winter.

9. Antarctica's dry, cold climate and unusually clear summer skies create excellent conditions for astrophysicists and other scientists.

Extend: Select a passage from your own writing. Identify both the simple and complete subjects and predicates. If you frequently write fragments or run-on sentences, this practice (finding the subjects and predicates) can help you identify and correct such errors.

© Houghton Mifflin Harcourt Publishing Company

TEKS 9.17C
ELPS 4C, 5E

Review: Subjects & Predicates

> **Expand** the simple subjects and predicates in the following sentences.

1. Parents hesitate.

My parents hesitate to give me advice about how to succeed in life.

2. Advice can be rejected.

_____

_____

3. She will vote in the next election.

_____

_____

4. Dogs bark.

_____

_____

5. Fireworks explode.

_____

_____

> **Write** three sentences using complete subjects and predicates. Circle the simple subjects and underline the simple predicates in the sentences you wrote. Draw a line between the complete subject and the complete predicate in each sentence.

1. _____

_____

2. _____

_____

3. _____

_____

© Houghton Mifflin Harcourt Publishing Company

TEKS 9.17A(i)
ELPS 4C

Pretest: Phrases

> **Identify** the underlined phrases using *G* for gerund, *I* for infinitive, *P* for participial, and *A* for appositive. Circle all the prepositional phrases. A prepositional phrase is often part of another kind of phrase. Study the first sentence to learn how to mark such constructions.

1. <u>Shaking *P* violently (from the cold,)</u> Janis couldn't wait outside any longer.
2. <u>To earn a grade based on effort</u> seemed fair to the students.
3. Leonardo da Vinci's famous painting, <u>*the Mona Lisa*</u>, portrays an unknown woman.
4. <u>Walking alone at night</u> is not safe.
5. The entire building, <u>the two shops and the bank</u>, was being renovated.
6. The town's safety codes about <u>renovating old structures</u> are outdated.
7. His empty stomach, <u>rumbling like an avalanche</u>, needed food.
8. The alarm clock told him it was time <u>to get up and work in the shop</u>.

> **Underline** and identify the phrases in the following sentences. Use the same symbols as above and circle the prepositional phrases.

1. In the game of baseball, stealing first base is impossible.
2. Why is it so hard to steal first base?
3. Raising the coffin's lid, Dracula, that scary monster, peered into the darkness at the other cloaked figures.
4. Weaving her way around the floating buoys, she swam to the boat.
5. Her face, puckered from age and countless worries, broke into a wide grin at the sight of her granddaughter.
6. To save the child, the paramedic performed CPR inside the wrecked automobile.
7. Feeding the birds is becoming a year-round activity.
8. Do you like to feed the birds?

© Houghton Mifflin Harcourt Publishing Company

 **TEKS** 9.17A(i)
ELPS 4C, 5E

Verbal Phrases

A verbal phrase is a phrase based on one of the three types of verbals: gerund, infinitive, or participle. Turn to 784.1 in *Write Source* for explanations and examples.

> **Name** the type of each underlined verbal phrase and tell how it is used in the sentence. Then compose a sentence using that type of verbal phrase.

1. Having caught the ball, he took off for the end zone.

  Participial phrase used as an adjective.

  Watching the horizon, I spotted the funnel cloud.

2. To cry at the movies is human.

_____

_____

3. I grew tired of his stomping around.

_____

_____

4. Smiling at everyone is one of her habits.

_____

_____

5. Ranting and raving about the poor rehearsal, the director stomped offstage.

_____

_____

6. Grandma baked raisin pie to please Grandpa.

_____

_____

Extend: Write three to five sentences about playing a game. Include at least one of the three types of verbal phrases in each sentence, and identify what kind it is.

© Houghton Mifflin Harcourt Publishing Company

ELPS 4C, 5E

Prepositional Phrases

A prepositional phrase consists of a preposition, its object, and any modifiers. Turn to pages 776 and 786 in *Write Source* for examples and more information.

> **Underline** the prepositional phrases below. Then circle each preposition and connect it to its object with an arrow. (Note: Sometimes "to" is part of an infinitive.)

1. Members of professional or recreational groups—from pilots to bowlers—often use special slang or technical words called *jargon.*

2. In the jargon of airline pilots, passengers may be called "geese."

3. To truckers—who have invented a lot of colorful slang through the years—an accelerator is a "hammer," and a state trooper is a "smokey."

4. Some slang comes from those who live in the shadowy underworld.

5. This special slang, known as *argot* or *cant,* is designed to protect criminals who might be overheard talking about their crimes.

6. The words "joint" (a cheap bar or restaurant) and "scram" (to get away quickly) came into our vocabulary from criminal jargon.

7. *Idioms* are special phrases whose meanings cannot be determined simply through the definitions of their individual words.

8. For example, consider the following idioms: "kick the bucket" (to die) and "up the creek" (in trouble).

9. Over the years, many slang words have become part of our standard language.

10. "Hairdo" was invented in the 1920s as a slang term for *coiffure,* but it became a standard word within 20 years.

11. Some slang terms are very old—"grub" (food) dates back to the 1600s and "lousy" (bad) dates from the 1700s.

Extend: Write three to five sentences about slang words or phrases that are popular at your school (no vulgarity allowed). Include at least one prepositional phrase in each sentence, and identify them with underlining.

© Houghton Mifflin Harcourt Publishing Company

ELPS 4C, 5E

Appositive Phrases

An appositive phrase, consisting of a noun and its modifiers, immediately follows another noun and renames it. Although the phrase adds new information, it functions as a noun and does not modify any word as an adjective would. Turn to 784.1 in *Write Source*.

Underline the appositive phrases in the following sentences.

1. The Internet, the world's largest computer network, became possible with the evolution of personal computers.

2. On the Net, information resources—national news services, stock reports, and libraries—can place a wealth of facts and details at your fingertips.

3. Newsgroups, a popular Internet destination, enable you to share ideas with people who are interested in a particular subject.

4. Abbe Don, "the electronic-storyteller-lady," conducts two digital storytelling projects on the Internet.

5. Digital storytelling, a rapidly growing phenomenon on the Internet, connects authors with their readers, who actually help develop the stories.

Practice writing appositive phrases. Add more information about each noun.

1. My mother, _____ , rode a horse in the parade.

2. My father, _____ , stood on the sidewalk and waved to her.

3. My little sister, _____ , told everyone, "That's my mother."

4. The mayor, _____ , rode a camel in the parade.

5. The parade, _____ , went down Main Street.

Extend: Read a page in one of your textbooks and count the number of appositive phrases you find. Are they used frequently? Do you use them in your writing?

© Houghton Mifflin Harcourt Publishing Company

 **TEKS** 9.17A(i)
ELPS 4C, 5E

Review: Phrases

> **Identify** each phrase. Write sentences using the following phrases: prepositional, appositive, infinitive, participial, and gerund.

1. in the hall _prepositional phrase_

We passed in the hall between classes.

_____

2. my favorite sport _____

_____

_____

3. driving the truck _____

_____

_____

4. to find the address _____

_____

_____

5. beyond the city limits _____

_____

_____

6. shattered into a thousand pieces _____

_____

_____

7. to keep trying _____

_____

_____

© Houghton Mifflin Harcourt Publishing Company

ELPS 4C

Pretest: Clauses

> **Underline** the independent clause once and the dependent clause twice in the following sentences.

1. She bicycled around the lake while the race was in progress.

2. After the cast took their bows, the curtain descended.

3. The pessimist sees a half-empty glass while the optimist notices it is half-full.

4. The ballpark's maintenance crew covered the diamond with a plastic tarp as soon as the umpire called the rain delay.

5. Though Morgan had been down the street many times before, he was not sure which house was Delphine's.

> **Circle** the noun clauses, underline the adverb clauses once, and underline the adjective clauses twice in the following sentences.

1. Although it wasn't a long speech, the coach's pep talk sparked her team to victory.

2. Nate skied down the mountain as if he were being chased.

3. The working time that falls between midnight and dawn is sometimes called the "graveyard shift."

4. What the father said as he walked her down the aisle made his daughter smile.

5. As long as you stay on Main Street, you can't miss it.

6. The quarterback, whose shoulder pads were twisted out of his jersey, blindly heaved the football toward the end zone.

7. Take out the garbage after you scrape all the plates.

8. You will never believe what Carolina did next.

© Houghton Mifflin Harcourt Publishing Company

 **TEKS** 9.17C
ELPS 4C, 5E, 5F

Independent & Dependent Clauses

A clause is a group of words that includes both a subject and a predicate. An independent clause presents a complete thought and can stand alone as a sentence. A dependent clause does not present a complete thought and cannot stand alone. Dependent clauses often begin with a subordinating conjunction or relative pronoun. Turn to 786.1–786.2 in *Write Source*.

> **Draw** one line under the independent clauses and two lines under the dependent clauses in the following sentences. Write *S* above each simple subject and *P* above each simple predicate.

1. <u>$\overset{S}{\text{Sleep}}$ $\overset{P}{\text{is}}$ a time of rest</u> <u><u>when the $\overset{S}{\text{sleeper}}$ $\overset{P}{\text{loses}}$ awareness of his or her surroundings.</u></u>

2. All human beings need sleep; only those who get enough high-quality sleep can perform at their best.

3. To study sleep, scientists use a machine called an electroencephalograph, which measures the electrical activity of the brain.

4. While people are relaxed and awake, their brains emit about 10 small electrical waves per second.

5. As they fall into a deep sleep, their brains emit slower and larger waves.

6. The slowest, largest waves occur during the first two or three hours of sleep, which is the phase known as "slow-wave sleep."

7. When they are dreaming, people's eyes move rapidly, and their brains emit small, fast waves.

8. Scientists call this dreaming phase "REM," which stands for "rapid eye movement."

9. During an eight-hour sleep, most people experience three to five periods of dreaming.

Extend: Circle the subordinating conjunctions and relative pronouns in the sentences above. Use these words in three to five sentences of your own. Each should contain both an independent and a dependent clause.

© Houghton Mifflin Harcourt Publishing Company

9.17C
ELPS 4C, 5E

Adverb, Adjective, & Noun Clauses

An adverb clause is used like an adverb, an adjective clause is used like an adjective, and a noun clause is used in place of a noun. Turn to 786.2 in *Write Source* for examples and more information.

> **Find** the dependent clauses in the following sentences, and underline and identify them. Use *ADV* for adverb clauses, *ADJ* for adjective clauses, and *N* for noun clauses.

1. What happens to a person <u>while he or she sleeps</u>? *ADV*

2. When a person falls asleep, all activity decreases and the muscles relax.

3. A sleeping person, who becomes less and less aware of what is happening around her or him, changes positions at least a dozen times.

4. Although some may shift their entire bodies, most sleepers move just their heads, arms, or legs.

5. While one experiences REM (rapid eye movement) sleep, the body cannot move.

6. This means that your body does not move during your dreams.

7. The pathways that carry nerve impulses from the brain to the muscles are blocked during REM sleep so that no movement can occur.

8. The cerebral cortex, which is the part of the brain involved in higher mental functions, is much more active during the dreaming state.

9. Dreams include places, situations, and feelings that the dreamer may have experienced.

10. Incidents that happen in the hours before sleep may appear in dreams.

11. In other words, what you dream is probably related to things that happen throughout the day prior to the dream.

12. Many experts who study dreams also believe that dreams are related to the deep wishes and fears of the dreamer.

Extend: Compose three sentences—one for each of the three types of clauses reviewed above. Exchange papers with a classmate and identify the clauses in each other's sentences.

© Houghton Mifflin Harcourt Publishing Company

TEKS 9.17C
ELPS 4C, 5E

Review: Clauses

> **Write** sentences following the directions below.

1. Write a sentence containing a dependent clause used as a noun.

_____

_____

2. Write a sentence containing a dependent clause used as an adjective.

_____

_____

3. Write a sentence containing a dependent clause used as an adverb.

_____

_____

4. Adjective clauses are introduced by _____ .

5. Adverb clauses are introduced by _____ .

> **Underline** the adjective and adverb clauses in the following sentences. Write *ADJ* above each adjective clause and *ADV* above each adverb clause.

1. Although most of Antarctica lies beneath snow and ice, sand dunes exist in the dry valleys of the Transantarctic Mountains.

2. Strong winds that blow the snow away before it can accumulate ripple the sand in Victoria Valley, one of the dry valleys.

3. Volcanoes that are found in West Antarctica are a part of a string of volcanoes in the Pacific Ocean known as the Ring of Fire.

4. Smoke drifts up from Mount Erebus because it is an active volcano.

© Houghton Mifflin Harcourt Publishing Company

ELPS 4C, 5B, 5E

Review: Phrase or Clause?

Describe on the lines below the difference between a phrase and a clause.

_____

_____

_____

Identify each group of words below. Use *P* for phrase and *C* for clause.

____ **1.** into the darkness

____ **2.** of Antarctica

____ **3.** winds blow the sand

____ **4.** volcanoes exist

____ **5.** of the brave scientists

____ **6.** at noon

____ **7.** to hunt seals and whales

____ **8.** researchers collect fossils

____ **9.** above sea level

____ **10.** temperatures plunge

Indicate whether the underlined portions of each of the sentences below are clauses or phrases. Use *C* for clause and *P* for phrase.

1. Antarctica has not always been buried <u>in ice</u>. *P*

2. <u>Millions of years ago</u>, <u>Antarctica was a much warmer place</u>.

3. Gondwanaland, a land mass <u>that included Antarctica, Africa, Australia, India, and South America</u>, began to break apart <u>about 140 million years ago</u>.

4. <u>Antarctica began drifting south</u>, and <u>ice began building up</u>.

5. This happened <u>approximately 30 million years ago</u>.

6. Evidence <u>that supports this finding</u> comes <u>from fossil studies</u>.

7. Antarctica is inhabited today <u>by a number of scientists</u>.

8. The scientists come from <u>many different nations</u>, yet <u>they all work together</u>.

© Houghton Mifflin Harcourt Publishing Company

ELPS 4C

Pretest: Sentences

> **Label** the following sentences: write *D* for declarative, *I* for interrogative, *IP* for imperative, *E* for exclamatory, or *C* for conditional. Add end punctuation.

_____ **1.** You can't be serious

_____ **2.** Please pass the salt

_____ **3.** The senior prom queen was also the school's valedictorian

_____ **4.** Have you ever fished before

_____ **5.** If the squirrel didn't work so hard in the fall, it wouldn't eat so well in the winter

_____ **6.** She just broke the world record

_____ **7.** Is there enough flour to make two loaves of bread

> **Write** *S* for simple, *CD* for compound, *CX* for complex, or *CD-CX* for compound-complex for each of the following sentences.

_____ **1.** Charity begins at home, but it would be nice if you did some community volunteer work, too.

_____ **2.** After I read the whole book, I finally understood its title.

_____ **3.** Although she worked hard for the promotion, she got it because of her strong people skills; however, she was disappointed when she found out she had to relocate.

_____ **4.** Hillary and Anya jogged around the track for 10 laps.

_____ **5.** Scottish terriers are solid black, and West Highland terriers are solid white.

_____ **6.** Wishful thinking won't get you any closer to your goals unless you also make a plan and follow it.

_____ **7.** The producer liked the recording; it reminded him of a cross between Will Smith and Garth Brooks.

_____ **8.** Now I understand the four kinds of sentences.

© Houghton Mifflin Harcourt Publishing Company

TEKS 9.17C
ELPS 4C, 5E, 5F

Basic Sentence Patterns

A sentence consists of a subject and a predicate and expresses a complete thought. Basic sentences follow certain patterns. If you use these patterns, your sentences will almost always be clear and correct. Study the examples below, and turn to page 800 in *Write Source*.

> **Judy ran.**
> (Subject + Action Verb [Predicate])

> **Josh ate carrots sticks.**
> (Subject + Action Verb + Direct Object)

> **Clowns give audiences enjoyment.**
> (Subject + Action Verb + Indirect Object + Direct Object)

> **The clown looks funny.**
> (Subject + Linking Verb + Predicate Adjective)

> **Ms. Maggie-Moo is a clown.**
> (Subject + Linking Verb + Predicate Noun)

Write a sentence for each pattern. Use the above examples for models.

1. Subject + Action Verb

_____

2. Subject + Action Verb + Direct Object

_____

3. Subject + Action Verb + Indirect Object + Direct Object

_____

4. Subject + Linking Verb + Predicate Adjective

_____

5. Subject + Linking Verb + Predicate Noun

_____

Extend: Now experiment with expanding the basic sentences you wrote above. Use the suggestions on page 606 in *Write Source*. When you can write a basic sentence, you are a writer. When you can expand a basic sentence, you are a better writer.

© Houghton Mifflin Harcourt Publishing Company

TEKS 9.17C
ELPS 4C, 5E, 5F

Kinds of Sentences

The four most common kinds of sentences are declarative, interrogative, imperative, and exclamatory. A fifth kind of sentence, conditional, expresses wishes ("if . . . then" statements). Turn to 788.1 in *Write Source*.

> **The history of golf still remains a mystery.** *(declarative)*

> **In what country did golf originate?** *(interrogative)*

> **Go to Scotland and find out.** *(imperative)*

> **Arnold Palmer did not invent golf!** *(exclamatory)*

> **If I ever get a hole in one, I'll dance on the green.** *(conditional)*

Identify the kind of sentence below by writing declarative, interrogative, imperative, exclamatory, or conditional in the blank. Add the appropriate end punctuation.

interrogative **1.** What changes have golf balls gone through**?**

_____ **2.** I can hardly believe the changes

_____ **3.** Golf balls have been made of wood, leather, and rubber

_____ **4.** Did you know that some balls have titanium cores

_____ **5.** Research continues in the hope that an improved design will enable golfers to hit golf balls farther

_____ **6.** If golf-ball design continues to improve, people will improve their scores

_____ **7.** Golf clubs have evolved, too

_____ **8.** Look at old clubs to see the differences

_____ **9.** Originally, golf clubs were made of wood

_____ **10.** In the 1920s, steel replaced wood

_____ **11.** What are they using today to make golf clubs

_____ **12.** Golf clubs are made out of graphite, titanium, and other metals

Extend: Write five sentences about a sport or hobby you're interested in. Each sentence should be a different kind.

© Houghton Mifflin Harcourt Publishing Company

 9.17C
ELPS 4C, 5E, 5F

Types of Sentences

A sentence may be *simple, compound, complex,* or *compound-complex* depending on the relationship between independent and dependent clauses. Turn to 790.1 in *Write Source* for more information and examples.

> **Label** each sentence below. Use **S** for simple, **CD** for compound, **CX** for complex, and **CD-CX** for compound-complex.

1   Do you know the theory of black holes? ___*S*___ Objects in space have

2   gravitational pull, so smaller objects are attracted to larger objects. ____

3   Throw a rock into the air, and it falls to earth when gravity pulls the rock

4   down. _____ Imagine throwing a rock so far and fast that it escapes the

5   earth's gravitational pull. _____ The exact speed necessary to escape

6   gravitational pull is called *escape velocity.* _____

7   Escape velocity and age contribute to the creation of black holes. _____

8   A large star grows old and can't withstand the force of its own gravity, so it

9   collapses. _____ The star collapses to a fraction of its former size, but its mass

10   and gravity remain the same. _____ A concentrated field of gravity is created

11   because the forces of mass and gravity stay strong despite the collapse, and a

12   black hole is formed. _____

13   With an escape velocity beyond light speed, a black hole prevents light from

14   escaping and this gives the black hole its name. _____ Replacing the name

15   "frozen star," John Archibald Wheeler coined the term "black hole." _____ You

16   can't escape a black hole unless you can travel faster than light, and man

17   cannot travel at such speeds. _____ The existence of black holes is difficult to

18   prove, but scientists continue trying. _____

Extend: Compose one of each of the four types of sentences. To double-check your work, label all the dependent and independent clauses in each sentence. For help, turn to 786.1 in *Write Source.*

© Houghton Mifflin Harcourt Publishing Company

TEKS 9.17C
ELPS 4C, 5E, 5F

Modeling a Sentence 1

Writing your own version of a sentence by a famous author, imitating it part by part, teaches you ways to put personality, rhythm, balance, and variety into your sentences. Turn to page 612 and 792.1 in *Write Source*.

> **Read** each sentence below and follow the directions to learn procedures for modeling sentences.

1. "Soon a glow began in the dark, a tiny circle barely red."

—Joseph Krumgold, *Onion John*

    a. Underline the main clause in the sentence above.

    b. Copy the prepositional phrase: _____.

    c. What word in the first part does the last part describe? _____

    d. Model the sentence above. Write a main clause, add a prepositional

        phrase, then add a detail that describes something in the main clause:

        _____

        _____

2. "Then, stomach down on the bed, he began to draw."

—Katherine Patterson, *Bridge to Terabithia*

    a. Underline the main clause in the sentence above.

    b. What part of speech introduces this sentence? _____

    c. Copy the prepositional phrase used in this sentence. _____

        _____

    d. What word in the main clause does the second part ("stomach down on the

        bed") describe? _____

    e. Model the sentence above: _____

        _____.

Extend: Find a sentence in a book or magazine that you think sounds especially good. Give it to a classmate to model.

© Houghton Mifflin Harcourt Publishing Company

 TEKS 9.17C
ELPS 4C, 5E, 5F

Modeling a Sentence 2

Writers often use specially designed sentences to emphasize a detail, to expand a thought, or to begin or end a piece of writing. They add various kinds of phrases and clauses to the main thought to create stylistic sentences. If you want to know the names for different stylistic sentences, turn to 792.1 in *Write Source*. This exercise will help you create stylistic sentences.

> **Model** the sentences below. If you have not modeled sentences before, use the suggestions on page 612 in *Write Source*. The main clause in each sentence is in italics.

1. On his stomach, an inch at a time, *he came to me and laid his head in my hand.*
               —Wilson Rawls, *Where the Red Fern Grows*

_____

_____

2. *There's still snow on the ground,* a dirty filigree, though the winter is losing its hardness and glitter.
               —Margaret Atwood, *Cat's Eye*

_____

_____

3. *Charles sat there on the floor of the corridor whimpering,* not a small boy's sound, but a fearful, animal noise.
            —Madeleine L'Engle, *A Wrinkle in Time*

_____

_____

4. *Then he turned and left,* a tired and bruised old man who somehow represented the pride and dignity of a whole race.
           —Hal Borland, *When the Legends Die*

_____

_____

_____

5. With his face burning and his head bowed, *he walked through court after court,* hearing that voice roaring ahead.
            —Pearl Buck, *The Good Earth*

_____

_____

_____

© Houghton Mifflin Harcourt Publishing Company

 **TEKS** 9.17C
ELPS 4C, 5E, 5F

Review: Sentences

> **Identify** the following sentences as either declarative, interrogative, imperative, exclamatory, or conditional. Add the correct end punctuation.

_____ **1.** I saw my brother take the remote control to his bedroom

_____ **2.** If you picked the color, then I should choose the shape

_____ **3.** What did you do with my new soccer ball

_____ **4.** That was a terrific shot

_____ **5.** Go home and take the roast out of the oven

> **Write** a stylistic sentence using the sentence below as a model. The main thought is in italics.

Or a tornado would twist down and do strange tricks to the things it hit, carrying someone fifty yards and leaving him barely hurt, or driving straws into car tires like needles. . . .
                                    —Willie Morris, _Good Old Boy_

_____

_____

_____

_____

> **Write** sentences that demonstrate the following structures.

1. (Simple) _____

2. (Compound) _____

_____

3. (Complex) _____

_____

© Houghton Mifflin Harcourt Publishing Company

Pretest: Subject-Verb Agreement

Underline the verb that agrees in number with its subject.

1. Neither he nor she *(is, are)* strong enough to lift the barbell.

2. The teacher as well as the students *(is, are)* required to attend the assembly.

3. Mathematics *(has, have)* always been my favorite subject.

4. Most of the picture *(was, were)* covered in blue and red paint.

5. There *(is, are)* disagreements among the committee members.

6. Some of the ice-cream cones in the pack *(was, were)* crushed.

7. Neither one of them *(is, are)* qualified to make that decision.

8. All of the collie's fur *(was, were)* knotted with burdocks.

9. Honesty and integrity *(was, were)* just two of Abraham Lincoln's most famous characteristics.

10. *Jack and the Beanstalk (is, are)* the first graders' favorite story.

11. There *(is, are)* more to their stories than either witness *(is, are)* willing to say.

12. The cleaners promised that his trousers *(was, were)* going to be cleaned, pressed, and delivered in time for the award ceremony.

13. The paper plates, napkins, and coleslaw *(was, were)* brought to the picnic by the Sungs.

14. It *(was, were)* the Crain family that *(was, were)* supposed to bring the ice and chicken.

15. None of the 3-D movies *(is, are)* much fun without the special glasses.

© Houghton Mifflin Harcourt Publishing Company

ELPS 4C, 5E

Subject-Verb Agreement 1

A verb must agree in number (singular or plural) with its subject. Study the examples below. Turn to pages 794–796 in *Write Source*.

> **A student sings the national anthem.** (*Student* and *sings* are both singular.)
>
> **Students sing the national anthem.** (*Students* and *sing* are both plural.)

Study the sentences below. Underline the subject and circle the correct verb.

---

1. <u>Cynthia Moss</u> *(study,* (*studies*)*)* and *(protect,* (*protects*)*)* elephants.

2. Her research *(have, has)* been done in Kenya's Amboseli National Park.

3. Moss *(is, are)* tracking more than 1,000 elephants.

4. Wild African elephants *(leads, lead)* extraordinary social lives.

5. Elephant families, made up of adult females and their young, *(is, are)* led by the oldest female of the group.

6. Each family *(rely, relies)* on this leader and her memory.

7. Life and death *(depend, depends)* on her skills during droughts when both food and water *(is, are)* scarce.

8. Katy Payne, who *(record, records)* songs of humpback whales, *(is, are)* helping Moss record elephant sounds.

9. Payne and Moss *(is, are)* learning what elephants *(says, say)* to each other.

10. Moss, who also *(protect, protects)* the elephants from poachers, *(say, says)* 85 percent of the world's wild elephants *(was, were)* killed between 1979 and 1989.

11. Tribal people, the Masai, *(helps, help)* her protect the elephants.

Extend: Write eight sentences, one for each verb in the following pairs: *is, are; attend, attends; know, knows; was, were.* Make your subjects and verbs agree.

© Houghton Mifflin Harcourt Publishing Company

ELPS 4C, 5E

Subject-Verb Agreement 2

> **Underline** the subjects and circle the correct verbs in the sentences below. All the subjects will be either plural nouns (turn to 748.1 and 762.1) or collective nouns (796.1).

1. The construction crew *(is, are)* continuing work on the new bridge.

2. The scissors *(is, are)* still missing.

3. The counseling committee *(was, were)* providing new services for students.

4. The rescue squad along with several police cars *(was, were)* at the scene of the accident almost immediately.

5. The crowd *(grows, grow)* restless before the musicians appear.

6. Mathematics *(is, are)* my favorite subject.

7. The news always *(is, are)* on at 6:00 p.m.

> **Underline** the subjects and circle the correct verbs in the sentences below. Some of the subjects will be indefinite (turn to 752.4) and relative pronouns (752.2).

1. Many of America's scenic highways *(curves, curve)* through mountains.

2. The scenic roads, which *(is, are)* found in all parts of America, *(requires, require)* alert drivers.

3. One, Highway 12 in Utah, *(makes, make)* you think of another planet.

4. Somebody who drives Highway 12 every day *(says, say)* everyone should drive it by the light of the full moon.

5. Some of Highway 12 *(passes, pass)* through vast open spaces.

6. Groups of visitors who *(travels, travel)* America's scenic highways *(thinks, think)* these roads are engineering marvels.

Extend: Compose five to eight sentences using plural and collective nouns and indefinite and relative pronouns. Make certain your subjects and verbs agree. Exchange papers with a classmate and check each other's work.

 **ELPS** 4C, 5E, 5F

Subject-Verb Agreement 3

> **Underline** the subjects and circle the correct verbs in the sentences below. Some of the subjects will be delayed (turn to 780.2).

1. There *(is, are)* a number of homeless cats at the Humane Society.

2. Whooping cranes *(is, are)* an endangered species.

3. Jackie's study habits *(is, are)* deplorable and distressing!

4. Here *(is, are)* the CD you left at my house yesterday.

5. *(Wasn't, Weren't)* Jen or George supposed to help you clean?

6. *(Has, Have)* the rain stopped yet?

7. There in the distance *(was, were)* the remains of the ghost town.

8. The tortoise *(is, are)* the animal with the longest life span.

> **Underline** the subjects and circle the correct verbs in the sentences below. Most of the subjects will be connected with conjunctions. Turn to 778.1–778.3.

1. Mike and Mary *(spend, spends)* most of their spare time fishing.

2. Both the bonfire and the canoe trip *(was, were)* the campers' favorite activities.

3. The bifocal lens and lightning rods *(was, were)* invented by Ben Franklin.

4. The forked tongue of the lizard and the snake *(is, are)* used to smell.

5. Neither Jim nor Earl *(complains, complain)* about mowing the grass.

6. The floor and the ceiling *(need, needs)* painting.

7. The floor or the ceiling *(needs, need)* painting.

8. Do you or I *(has, have)* the house keys?

Extend: Choose a hobby you enjoy. Write three to five sentences joining subjects with conjunctions. Write several sentences using a linking verb. Also try to write at least one sentence with a delayed subject. Be sure your subjects agree with your verbs.

© Houghton Mifflin Harcourt Publishing Company

ELPS 4C

Review: Subject-Verb Agreement

> **Underline** the subjects and circle the correct verbs in the sentences below.

1. Deep-sea diving equipment *(gives, give)* individuals the ability to explore a vast underwater world.

2. Two main techniques for diving *(is, are)* diving with a JIM suit or diving with a helmet.

3. Marine geologists and biologists *(uses, use)* these two techniques.

4. Around the corner *(is, are)* several fresh footprints in the cement.

5. Cindy or Jose *(was, were)* in charge of the food drive.

6. None of his friends *(wants, want)* to see Javier move away.

7. All of the senators *(wants, want)* the president to call a special session.

8. The clean-up committee *(tries, try)* to keep the sidewalks clean.

9. Here *(is, are)* the books that you ordered from the book club.

10. The dolphins *(is, are)* following our boat.

11. One of the preschoolers *(is, are)* crying.

12. Many of the preschoolers *(is, are)* crying.

13. The neon lights *(was, were)* lighting up the whole street.

14. Two of the couples *(was, were)* waiting for the bus.

15. Often families *(is, are)* separated during a war.

16. Both the toy and the granola bar *(is, are)* for you.

17. Both of the editors *(has, have)* proofread the next chapter.

18. There *(is, are)* in the closet a pair of cross-country skis.

19. Few of the wolves *(kills, kill)* cattle.

20. Not one of the wolves *(kills, kill)* cattle.

© Houghton Mifflin Harcourt Publishing Company

ELPS 4C

Pretest: Pronoun-Antecedent Agreement

Underline the pronouns and draw an arrow to each antecedent. If a pronoun does not agree with its antecedent, cross out the pronoun and write the correct pronoun above.

1. Ella made sure her roller skates fit correctly before taking ~~it~~ *them* to the rink.

2. The politicians had made up his minds long before the bill made its way out of the committee.

3. The stockbrokers on the trading-room floor had their arms up, yelling words that made the traders sound like we were from a foreign country.

4. If Jerrill wants this project done right, he will have to do them himself.

5. Mia and her soccer team won her match with Franklin High to win the city tournament.

6. The baseball was signed by Grady Sizemore after he clobbered it into the right-field bleachers.

7. Was the accountant driving a company car to her meeting?

8. The president had already served two terms, so he was not eligible to run for the presidency again.

9. The radio station ran their yearly contest to see if listeners could correctly name a few old songs.

10. The king and their court moved from the castle to his stronghold in the East.

11. I, George Washington, cannot tell a lie; I cut down the cherry tree with our little hatchet.

12. No worker is required to pay for their own transportation.

© Houghton Mifflin Harcourt Publishing Company

ELPS 4C, 5E

Pronoun-Antecedent Agreement 1

Pronouns must agree in number and gender with their antecedents, the words to which the pronouns refer. Turn to page 798 in *Write Source*.

> **Underline** the antecedent for each pair of pronouns below; then choose the pronoun that agrees in number with its antecedent. Write that pronoun on the line provided. For an indefinite pronoun (like "everyone") use the phrase "his or her" or "her or his."

1. <u>Each</u> of the female runners in the race bettered *(her, their)* previous best time.   *her*

2. Not everyone should include a four-year college in *(his or her, their)* future.   _____

3. Both of the girls told *(her, their)* parents about the dance.   _____

4. The team has chosen Waldo as *(its, their)* mascot.   _____

5. Many of Jack's errors reveal *(his, their)* lack of practice.   _____

6. Can anybody do this worksheet correctly without *(his or her, their)* handbook?   _____

7. The assembly voted to raise *(its, their)* salaries by 10 percent.   _____

8. Has anybody gotten *(her or his, their)* parents to chaperone the dance?   _____

9. Either Ramona or Christine will have to bring *(her, their)* toboggan if we hope to have enough room for everyone.   _____

10. No one going on the trip needs to bring *(his or her, their)* own lunch.   _____

11. If Carmen budgets time carefully, *(she, they)* will have little trouble finding time for both work and play.   _____

12. If you find my notes or outline, please bring *(it, them)* to me.   _____

13. Mario and Paulo showed slides of *(his, their)* home in Brazil.   _____

14. The players and manager were asked to give *(her or his, their)* predictions about the coming season.   _____

15. Either the drummer or the tuba player left *(his or her, their)* sheet music in the band room.   _____

Extend: Write a sentence for each of the following words, and make each pronoun agree with its antecedent: *each, any, everybody, none,* and *one.*

© Houghton Mifflin Harcourt Publishing Company

ELPS 4C, 5E

Pronoun-Antecedent Agreement 2

> **Circle** the correct pronoun and underline its antecedent.

1. Has either <u>Toya</u> or <u>Heather</u> remembered *(their, (her))* backpack?

2. Everyone on the girls' team discovered *(her, their)* own special strengths.

3. In all the excitement, one of the first contestants lost *(their, his or her)* shoes.

4. Somebody must have completely lost *(her or his, their)* mind!

5. When Amber left the cafeteria, *(they, she)* must have forgotten her backpack.

6. Neither Jordan nor his parents wanted *(his, their)* dessert.

7. Every dog has *(its, their)* day.

8. If Tina, Lena, or Sabrina would visit us, *(they, she)* would have a big surprise.

9. Because of a soccer player's schedule, *(he or she, they)* cannot run cross-country.

10. Even after a long debate, the student senate could not make up *(their, its)* mind.

11. Either Mr. Green or Mr. Slade backed *(their, his)* car into the sculpture.

12. Max and Ali were very concerned about *(his, their)* hair loss.

13. Each woman in the room had completed *(their, her)* questionnaire.

14. Many people cannot express *(their, his or her)* true feelings.

15. Will anyone come forward and claim *(her or his, their)* prize?

16. Because of all the uncertainty, nobody dared to offer *(their, his or her)* opinion.

17. Each of the academic teams had *(its, their)* own human computer.

18. Someone tell Kent or Chantal to bring *(their, his or her)* soccer ball tomorrow.

19. Both of the returning travelers are eager to describe *(her, their)* trip.

20. When I locate your black jacket or your down coat, I will send *(it, them)* to you.

Extend: Write sentences using each of these pronouns: *his, her, them, theirs, he, she, it, you, they.* Be certain to also include antecedents for the pronouns. Exchange papers with a classmate and check each other's sentences for pronoun-antecedent agreement.

© Houghton Mifflin Harcourt Publishing Company

ELPS 4C

Review: Pronoun-Antecedent Agreement

> **Underline** each pronoun's antecedent in the following paragraphs and circle the correct pronoun.

1   The members of our high school track team have chosen *(its, their)* mascot

2   for the coming year. Each member was involved in the selection process and

3   was able to voice *(his or her, their)* opinion. A committee first narrowed

4   *(its, their)* choices to three animals: a greyhound, a cheetah, and an opossum.

5   The opossum was the first candidate to lose its standing by a majority vote.

6   Each of the other candidates had *(its, their)* strong points, but in the end, the

7   greyhound won.

8   Next, we had to name *(our, their)* new mascot. The team voted to name

9   *(its, their)* mascot Wilbur. Wilbur has already charmed everyone into bringing

10   *(his or her, their)* leftovers to him. If you should wander into the locker room on

11   the day of a meet, don't be shocked to find Wilbur taking a shower with the

12   rest of the team. As far as Wilbur is concerned, *(it's, he's)* human.

13   Everyone who knows Wilbur loves *(her, him)*. From *(their, his)* wet, cold

14   nose to *(his, their)* furiously wagging tail, Wilbur is a bundle of joy. Even the

15   coach's family, famous for *(their, its)* cat lovers, have changed *(its, their)* tune.

16   They have adopted Wilbur and have given him a place to sleep in *(its, their)*

17   kitchen. Wilbur, of course, has other accommodations in mind; he's been seen

18   napping on *(its, his)* favorite spot—the Perez's sofa.

© Houghton Mifflin Harcourt Publishing Company

ELPS 4C, 5E, 5F

Pretest: Sentence Combining

Combine the following sentences. You may want to use the method in parentheses.

1. The Berlin Wall was built in 1961. It was about 42 kilometers (26 miles) long. *(Use a relative pronoun.)*

_____

_____

_____

2. The wall divided a city into two distinctly different communities. The city was Berlin, East Germany. *(Use an appositive.)*

_____

_____

_____

3. Communist East Berlin built the wall to prevent its citizens from emigrating to West Berlin. East Berlin was backed by the Soviet Union. *(Use an introductory phrase.)*

_____

_____

_____

4. The wall was constructed of 15-foot-high concrete slabs. It made escape to West Berlin extremely difficult. *(Use a participial phrase.)*

_____

_____

_____

5. Armed guards and guard dogs were used to secure the wall. Barbed wire, trenches, and electric alarms were also used. *(Use a series.)*

_____

_____

© Houghton Mifflin Harcourt Publishing Company

ELPS 4C, 5E, 5F

6. More than 170 people died trying to cross the wall. Most of them were killed by the border guards. *(Use a semicolon.)*

_____

_____

_____

7. In 1989, more freedom was demanded by East Germans. They wanted the freedom to emigrate and the freedom to travel. *(Use a key word.)*

_____

_____

_____

8. By 1990, demolition of the wall was well under way. The unification of East and West Germany was also taking place. *(Use correlative conjunctions.)*

_____

_____

_____

© Houghton Mifflin Harcourt Publishing Company

 **ELPS** 4C, 5E, 5F

Sentence Combining 1

Combining some of your simple sentences can result in variety, a characteristic of good writing. Here are some ways to combine sentences. Also see pages 607–608 in *Write Source*.

> **Practice** combining the following simple sentences. Try to use as many ways to combine sentences as you can. Label each sentence with the combining method you used.

1. (1) One of the mountains in the Teton Range is Grand Teton. (2) Another mountain is Mount Owen. (3) A third mountain is Mount Moran.

Mountains in the Teton Range include Grand Teton, Mount Owen, and Mount

Moran. (series)

2. (1) One bird of prey in the Tetons is the osprey. (2) Ospreys have superb fishing skills. (3) Ospreys are dark brown and white.

_____

_____

_____

3. (1) Buffalo are the largest land mammals in the United States. (2) Overhunting and mindless slaughter almost wiped out the buffalo.

_____

_____

_____

4. (1) Coyotes contribute to the Teton/Yellowstone ecosystem by eating mice, voles, and ground squirrels. (2) This keeps the rodent population under control.

_____

_____

_____

© Houghton Mifflin Harcourt Publishing Company

ELPS 4C, 5E, 5F

5. (1) River otters live along the streams in Grand Teton National Park. (2) They are weasel-like mammals. (3) They have short legs and webbed feet.

_____

_____

_____

_____

6. (1) Trumpeter swans live in Grand Teton National park during the winter. (2) They live throughout Canada during the summer. (3) They hatch their young in Canada during the summer.

_____

_____

_____

_____

7. (1) A number of moose live in Grand Teton National Park. (2) Their long legs and wide hooves make it easy for them to move through swamplands. (3) They also make it easy for them to walk through deep snow.

_____

_____

_____

_____

Extend: Use the sentences you wrote to form a paragraph about the animals and birds that live in Grand Teton National Park. Follow the guidelines on page 607–608 in _Write Source_. You may choose to re-combine some of the sentences in order to create a clear paragraph.

© Houghton Mifflin Harcourt Publishing Company

 ELPS 4C, 5E, 5F

Sentence Combining 2

Writing that contains too many short sentences often seems choppy and immature. To correct this problem, you can combine some of the sentences to create a variety of sentence lengths and types. Turn to pages 607–608 in *Write Source*.

> **Combine** the short sentences in each group below to create a single, more effective sentence. (You may edit the text as long as the basic meaning remains unchanged.)

1. Bees build amazingly strong honeycombs. The walls are only 1/80 inch thick. These walls can support 30 times their own weight.

    Bees build amazingly strong honeycombs; although the walls are only 1/80

    inch thick, they can support 30 times their own weight.

    _____

2. A bee colony contains from 50 to 60,000 bees. They are made up of workers, drones, and one queen bee.

    _____

    _____

    _____

3. Some bees are just 1/12 inch long. Some grow to be as long as an inch.

    _____

    _____

    _____

4. It takes a great deal of work for bees to make a pound of honey. They must travel a combined distance of 13,000 miles. This is about four times the distance across the United States.

    _____

    _____

    _____

Extend: Rewrite each of your sentences, combining the parts in another way.

© Houghton Mifflin Harcourt Publishing Company

ELPS 4C, 5E, 5F

Review: Sentence Combining

Use at least 10 of the facts listed below in five (or fewer) sentences. How you combine ideas is entirely up to you, but try to vary the combining methods you use.

Ravens
- appear to be serious birds
- are very playful
- are related to jays and magpies
- have fantastic memories
- have a wingspan of four feet
- mate for life
- live in stable flocks
- are related to crows
- are highly intelligent
- like to do midair acrobatics
- can recognize a gun from a great distance
- can learn to count
- know 60 different birdcalls
- can remember more than 1,000 hiding places for food

1. _____

_____

_____

2. _____

_____

_____

3. _____

_____

_____

4. _____

_____

_____

5. _____

_____

_____

© Houghton Mifflin Harcourt Publishing Company

TEKS 9.17C, 9.18B
ELPS 5F

Pretest: Sentence Problems

Correct the comma splices in the following sentences. (One sentence is correct.)

1. The conveyor belt was not working properly, it fed the parts to the assemblers too fast.

2. Casually whistling a tune, the tow-truck driver hooked up the car, it was parked illegally in a handicapped space.

3. Thundering through the narrow canyon, the wild mustangs instinctively knew that wranglers were close behind.

Rewrite the following sentences to correct any dangling modifiers.

1. Wildly flapping its miniature wings, the heavy tomcat stalked the baby robin.

The heavy tomcat stalked the baby robin, which was wildly flapping its

miniature wings.

2. Trying to swallow a wad of bubble gum, the teacher peered suspiciously at the student.

_____

_____

3. Barry picked up the injured bird who had compassion for all living things.

_____

_____

4. Tiptoeing gracefully across the stage, the director enjoyed watching the ballet dancers.

_____

_____

© Houghton Mifflin Harcourt Publishing Company

Cross out any double negatives or nonstandard language in the following sentences. **Write any necessary corrections above.**

1. If you will just wait up, I will be ready in a moment.

2. She hadn't scarcely made it through the door when the dog jumped into her arms.

3. Mandy and Roberto went off to do research for their social-studies project.

4. Try to save your money so you can go with next time.

5. The teacher should of let us use our notes on the test.

6. Try and get it right the first time, okay?

7. Don't use none of the warped boards.

Correct the fragments and rambling and run-on sentences in the passage below. **Besides correcting punctuation, you may add, delete, or rearrange words as necessary.**

1   Nancy snuggled deeper under the blanket and smiled because of her

2   pleasant dream, and turned over and managed to crack open one eye to   *She*

3   peek at the clock. Eight o'clock! Both of Nancy's eyelids snapped open. The

4   chapter 7 trigonometry test. This morning!

5   She raced to the bathroom, grabbed her toothbrush and toothpaste,

6   and leaned over to turn on the shower pressing a glob of paste onto the

7   brush, she tossed the toothpaste tube back toward the sink and it bounced

8   off and landed on the floor. Nancy stepped on the tube. Toothpaste

9   squirting between her toes and onto the bath mat.

10   So far, the morning was a real disaster. Didn't look like it was going

11   to improve any time soon. A broken hair dryer, a lost shoe, and a missing

12   button. What else could go wrong?

© Houghton Mifflin Harcourt Publishing Company

 TEKS 9.17C, 9.18B
ELPS 5F

Comma Splices & Run-On Sentences 1

A comma splice is a sentence error that results when two independent clauses are joined together with only a comma. A run-on sentence is a sentence error that results when two independent clauses are joined without any punctuation. Both of these errors can be corrected in one of several ways. Turn to page 609 in *Write Source*.

> **Place** an *RO* in front of each run-on sentence, a *CS* in front of each comma splice, and a *C* in front of each correct sentence. Correct each faulty sentence. Use the proofreading marks inside the back cover of *Write Source*.

_CS_ **1.** I never really enjoyed science, math is my favorite subject.

_____ **2.** By the time we arrived, the show was nearly over, we missed everything but the credits and the cartoon.

_____ **3.** Don't touch that chair it has just been painted.

_____ **4.** I got an "A" on my English test. I've never gotten one before.

_____ **5.** Some students would rather goof around than study, some adults went through the same thing when they were in school.

_____ **6.** Some run-on sentences are easy to recognize, others are much more difficult.

_____ **7.** Joan's mother works at the hospital her father works at the school.

_____ **8.** John had to go to his violin lesson, however, he will stop by when he is through.

_____ **9.** Katrin enjoys shopping for clothes, especially when someone else is paying for them.

_____ **10.** Time goes slowly when you are working, it seems to fly when you are playing.

_____ **11.** Akira will meet us at the skating rink later; he has to go home to pick up his skates.

Extend: Write two run-on sentences and two sentences with a comma splice. Exchange papers with a classmate and correct each other's sentence errors.

© Houghton Mifflin Harcourt Publishing Company

 TEKS 9.17C, 9.18B
ELPS 5F

Comma Splices & Run-On Sentences 2

There are three basic ways to correct comma splices and run-ons: (1) use a comma and a coordinating conjunction, (2) use a semicolon, or (3) make the clauses into separate sentences. Turn to page 609 in *Write Source*.

Correct the following sentences by inserting a semicolon, a period and a capital letter, or a comma and a coordinating conjunction. Use each method at least twice.

1. Psychology is the science that studies all kinds of behavior. *T*he behavior may be normal, *or* the behavior may be abnormal.

2. Psychologists try to find answers to questions about thoughts, feelings, and actions and their findings help us understand why people behave as they do.

3. In the late 1800s, psychology developed into a science based on observation and experimentation prior to that, there were no systematic studies of the mind.

4. Sigmund Freud introduced the theory that behavior is determined by the unconscious mind he developed techniques to uncover repressed feelings.

5. Many psychologists disagree with some of Freud's ideas most accept that the unconscious has a major effect on behavior.

6. Cognitive psychologists concentrate on thinking processes and self-awareness, they believe there's more to human nature than a response to a stimulus.

7. Humanistic psychologists trust that people's values and choices affect their behavior they believe the psychologist helps people to realize their unique possibilities.

8. Understanding of individuals and groups has broadened because of these psychological studies, the insights from these studies can benefit people in their everyday lives.

Extend: Write three run-on sentences about whatever you believe influences your behavior. Exchange papers with a classmate and correct each other's work.

© Houghton Mifflin Harcourt Publishing Company

TEKS 9.17C
ELPS 5F

Comma Splices & Run-On Sentences 3

Another way to revise a run-on sentence or a comma splice is to restructure the sentence. If one of the independent clauses is less important than the other, change it into a subordinate clause or a phrase. Turn to page 609 and 786.1 and 786.2 in *Write Source*.

> **Correct** the following sentences by using subordinate clauses or phrases.

1. An airship is different from a manned balloon it has an engine and steering equipment.

An airship, which is different from a manned balloon, has an engine and

steering equipment.

2. The main body of an airship is a balloon filled with a lighter-than-air gas, the gas raises the airship and keeps it in the air.

_____

_____

3. A series of explosions was caused by the hydrogen gas used in airships, this led to the use of helium gas in United States craft in the 1920s.

_____

_____

_____

4. Airships were also called dirigibles, zeppelins, or blimps they were used in World War I as bombers and as cargo and passenger carriers.

_____

_____

5. The *Hindenburg* was one of the largest airships ever built it exploded when its hydrogen gas somehow ignited, killing 36 people.

_____

_____

Extend: Write three run-on sentences about airplanes or air travel. Exchange papers with a classmate or work together. Experiment with a variety of ways to correct each sentence.

© Houghton Mifflin Harcourt Publishing Company

★ TEKS 9.17C

Sentence Fragments 1

A fragment is a group of words often mistaken for a sentence. A fragment is either a phrase or a dependent clause that looks or sounds like a sentence. Remember: A sentence contains a subject and a predicate and expresses a complete thought. Turn to page 610 in *Write Source*.

> **Complete Sentence:**
> The polar bear is a curious animal.

> **Fragments:**
> **Can be quite a clown** (subject missing)
> **When the bear is safely confined** (dependent clause, not a complete thought)
> **Of captive bears exceeding 1,000 pounds** (both subject and predicate missing)

Identify the following groups of words by writing *S* for sentence or *F* for fragment on the line before each. Put periods at the end of all sentences.

_S_ **1.** The polar bear is a large carnivore that does not fear humans.

____ **2.** Deliberately stalks and kills humans for food

____ **3.** Has been called the "King of the North"

____ **4.** When wounded, the polar bear can be a deadly adversary

____ **5.** Covered 60 yards in a charge after being shot through the heart several times

____ **6.** On the other hand, this bear can bring delight to its viewers

____ **7.** Once a coast guard vessel in the Canadian Arctic received a visit from an adult male polar bear

____ **8.** The bear, traveling atop a drifting ice floe

____ **9.** The crew, who did not know better, decided to feed the curious critter floating alongside the boat

____ **10.** A case of black molasses from the ship's storeroom

____ **11.** Soon the bear and the ice floe were black and sticky with the sweet stuff

____ **12.** After the molasses came the apples

Extend: Make each of the five sentence fragments into a complete sentence. Always proofread your writing for sentence fragments.

© Houghton Mifflin Harcourt Publishing Company

TEKS 9.17C

Sentence Fragments 2

Fragments, once found, need to be changed into sentences that contain a subject and a predicate and express a complete thought. Turn to page 610 in *Write Source*.

> **Make** the following fragments into complete sentences. Use the appropriate end punctuation.

1. Henry "Hank" Aaron, baseball's career home-run record holder for 33 years by hitting a total of 755 homers

Hitting a total of 755 homers, Henry "Hank" Aaron was baseball's career

home-run record holder for 33 years.

2. broke Babe Ruth's record—714 homers—in 1974

3. playing professionally for all-black teams when drafted by the Milwaukee Braves

4. with a lifetime batting average of .305 and 2,297 runs batted in and led the National League four times in runs batted in

5. the National League's most valuable player in 1957, elected to the Baseball Hall of Fame in 1982

6. as a right fielder won three Gold Glove awards for his fielding skills

© Houghton Mifflin Harcourt Publishing Company

Rambling Sentences

Rambling sentences go on and on, and readers can find them confusing. Overusing the word *and* is one cause. Turn to page 610 in *Write Source*.

Rewrite the following sentences so they are clear. Sometimes you may need to divide a rambling sentence into two sentences, or you may need to reword portions. Experiment with a variety of correction methods.

1. I took a trip to the Apostle Islands and they are in Lake Superior and getting there was both exciting and scary and we crossed some very choppy water.

I took a trip to the Apostle Islands in Lake Superior. Getting there was both

exciting and scary because we crossed some very choppy water.

_____

2. I went kayaking with a friend known as Frederick the Great Fisher, so we brought our fishing supplies, our maps and some food and tents and mosquito repellent and camped near Lake Superior.

_____

_____

_____

3. We paddled to Oak Island and Sand Island and we hiked on the trails and saw three deer and we ate lunch on the beach and went swimming afterward.

_____

_____

_____

4. After swimming we tried fishing but even Frederick the Great Fisher didn't catch anything so we put the kayaks into the water and paddled back to camp and complained about having to eat bologna for supper again.

_____

_____

_____

_____

Extend: Write one long rambling sentence about a fishing or swimming experience. Show two different ways to rewrite the sentence so it is clear.

© Houghton Mifflin Harcourt Publishing Company

 **TEKS** 9.17C, 9.18B
ELPS 5F

Review: Sentence Problems 1

Identify the sentence errors below by writing *F* for fragment, *RO* for run-on, *CS* for comma splice, and *R* for rambling. Change the sentences so that they are complete and effective.

_____ **1.** We are in the midst of the computer revolution even our cars are computerized.

_____

_____

_____ **2.** Computers can make life easier by doing our everyday tasks and helping us buy groceries and pump gas and do banking.

_____

_____

_____ **3.** Computer technology changes almost daily and thousands of creative minds are at work and new uses for computers are found.

_____

_____

_____ **4.** Overwhelmed by all this new technology.

_____

_____

_____ **5.** When considering the latest developments in the personal computer.

_____

_____

_____ **6.** The first computers were giant machines housed in special air-conditioned rooms, now they are often tiny machines, we carry them in our pockets.

_____

_____

© Houghton Mifflin Harcourt Publishing Company

Misplaced Modifiers

When a modifier is incorrectly placed in a sentence, the meaning of the sentence becomes confusing. This type of writing error is called a misplaced modifier. Generally the way to fix a misplaced modifier is to reorganize the sentence so that the modifier clearly describes or modifies the correct item. Turn to page 611 in *Write Source* for more information.

> **Rewrite** each sentence so that the modifier clearly modifies the correct word.

1. Jana bought four tickets for the concert this weekend at the grocery store.

  Jana bought four tickets at the grocery store for the concert this weekend.

  _____

2. Shavonn walked into a class that was discussing bookkeeping by mistake.

  _____

  _____

3. The flight attendants served cookies to the passengers after warming them.

  _____

  _____

4. Maryjean made computer greeting cards using a special software program personalized for her friends.

  _____

  _____

5. The student council has been planning to hold a pizza sale for two months.

  _____

  _____

6. The school needs someone to clean the cafeteria badly.

  _____

  _____

Extend: Write three to five sentences containing misplaced modifiers. Exchange papers with a classmate and correct each other's work.

© Houghton Mifflin Harcourt Publishing Company

Dangling Modifiers

When a modifying phrase or clause does not clearly and sensibly modify a word in a sentence, the result is called a dangling modifier. Dangling modifiers are difficult to recognize, especially in your own writing, but they are often easy to fix. Turn to page 611 in *Write Source*.

> **Fix** the dangling modifiers. Follow the suggested method given in parentheses.

1. Upon entering the science lab, the dangling skeleton caught my eye. *(Use "I" somewhere in this sentence.)*

As I entered the science lab, the dangling skeleton caught my eye.

_____

2. After pouring the coffee, her dog jumped on one of Grandma's guests. *(Name the person doing the acting in the introductory clause.)*

_____

_____

3. Having had three teeth knocked out, mother suggested that Josh quit the soccer team. *(Create a relative clause.)*

_____

_____

4. Using a computer to help diagnose engine problems, our car was repaired by Omar. *(Name a person as the subject.)*

_____

_____

5. Just after eating lunch, a strange-looking bird landed on our windowsill. *(Name a person as the subject.)*

_____

_____

Extend: Select two sentences from the exercise above and fix the dangling modifiers using a different method.

© Houghton Mifflin Harcourt Publishing Company

Wordiness & Deadwood

Make your sentences more concise by eliminating unnecessary or redundant words. Also see page 44 in *Write Source*.

> **Place** parentheses around the unnecessary words or phrases in the following sentences.

1. The former tenant (who had lived in the apartment before we moved in) had painted all the walls (with a coat of) pink (paint).

2. A typical basketball court is normally 90 feet long.

3. The main reason he didn't pass the test is because he didn't study his notes carefully or look over his notebook.

4. There are six students who volunteered on their own to clean up after the homecoming dance is over.

5. The injured climber was unable to descend down the mountain by himself, so he relied on the help of another climber to assist him.

6. The fragile vase, which would surely break if mishandled, was shipped "Special Handling" so that it would be handled with care.

7. The cancelled game has been rescheduled for 8:00 p.m. tomorrow evening.

8. A portable radio can be carried anywhere and is especially handy to use when jogging, biking, or doing other outdoor activities.

9. As a general rule, he usually spends about one hour of his time reading each day.

10. Needless to say, wordiness is a writing problem that should be eliminated from all writing, which goes without saying.

Extend: Carefully read a paper you have written. Put parentheses around unnecessary words and phrases. Read your revised work to a classmate. In your opinion, is your paper better now?

© Houghton Mifflin Harcourt Publishing Company

ELPS 1G, 5E

Nonstandard Language

Nonstandard English is not recommended for formal writing. Consider both your subject and your audience before deciding to use formal or informal language. Turn to page 611 in *Write Source*.

> **Cross out** the nonstandard language and double negatives in the sentences below. Write a correction, when needed, above the words. (Two sentences are correct as written.)

1. Not long ago, a team of divers went ~~off~~ to Texas to explore the Gulf of Mexico.

2. They wanted to locate a certain sunken ship.

3. It had settled in at a 12-foot depth and was covered with silt.

4. They didn't barely know where to begin.

5. The public believed the team didn't have no idea where that ship was at.

6. They had begun diving when one diver yelled, "Sharks!"

7. They thought they had went and did it this time.

8. You should of seen them try to get back to the boat!

9. The divers had not done nothing to protect themselves from sharks.

10. Man, oh man, they should of taken precautions.

11. "I would of enjoyed this expedition except for the sharks," one of the divers said.

12. Another diver said, "We won't never forget this day."

13. "I was so scared I couldn't hardly swim," said the youngest diver.

14. He added, "Don't never let no one convince you that diving has no hazards."

15. Evidently the sharks were not hardly man-eaters, for they swam away.

16. Meanwhile, a storm almost sank the divers' vessel—like freaky, man!

17. The divers went home, but next time they go exploring, I plan to go with.

Extend: Can you name any fictional characters who use nonstandard language? Select a passage in which a character speaks nonstandard English and rewrite it using formal language. What happens?

© Houghton Mifflin Harcourt Publishing Company

ELPS 4C, 5E

Unparallel Construction 1

Parallelism is the repetition of similar patterns or word groups—either words, phrases, or clauses—within a sentence. Turn to pages 602 in *Write Source*.

> **We went *to the park, to the game,* and *to the dance.***
> (The repetition of the prepositional phrases creates parallel structure.)

> **The dog *ran to the fence, jumped in the air,* and *barked at the squirrels.***
> (In this sentence, the repeated pattern is an action verb + a prepositional phrase.)

Underline the parallel parts of the sentences below. Then explain what word groups are repeated in each sentence.

1. I think that <u>I should get some juice</u>, <u>you should make the pizza</u>, and <u>Marie</u>

<u>should decorate the house.</u>

The repeated word group is a clause with a subject + an action verb + a

direct object. Also, each clause contains the word "should."

2. I met someone who could ride a unicycle, juggle three balls, and whistle "The

Star-Spangled Banner" at the same time.

_____

_____

3. At age 12, it seems our dog is either eating or sleeping.

_____

_____

4. When you turn 16, pass a math class, and stop bugging your little sister, we

will talk about getting a car for you.

_____

_____

Extend: Write two sentences that show examples of parallel structure. Have a classmate identify what types of word groups are repeated in each sentence.

© Houghton Mifflin Harcourt Publishing Company

ELPS 4C, 5E

Unparallel Construction 2

Parallel structuring is the repetition of similar words, phrases, or clauses. Inconsistent (unparallel) construction occurs when the kinds of words, phrases, or clauses change in the middle of a sentence. Turn to page 602 in *Write Source*.

Underline the parallel structures in the following sentences. Then write sentences using similar constructions.

1. Hamlet wondered whether <u>to live</u> or <u>to die</u>.

Jeremy wondered whether to play football or to join band.

2. Give me a day with sunshine and a strong wind, with a boat and a mended sail, with a lake and a distant horizon.

_____

_____

3. This is the dress, the hat, and the mask I will wear to the costume dance.

_____

_____

4. In the little town where I grew up, people pass the time chatting in the post office, walking the trails by the river, and counting the deer in the woods.

_____

_____

5. Benjamin Franklin was not only an inventor but also a statesman.

_____

_____

6. Walking strengthens your legs, swimming develops your lungs, and trusting expands your heart.

_____

_____

© Houghton Mifflin Harcourt Publishing Company

★ ELPS 4C, 5E

Follow the directions below to create sentences with parallel structures.

1. Complete the sentence using a series. Each part of the series should contain a past tense verb followed by a prepositional phrase.

Mr. Ortego was the kind of person who *arose at six, ate at seven, and left*

at eight.

2. Complete the sentence using a series of phrases.

To be a great point guard you need to be able to _____

_____

3. Complete the sentence using a series of clauses.

He was worried that _____

_____

_____

4. Complete the sentence using a series of prepositional phrases.

Somehow Breanne got paint _____

_____

5. Complete the sentence using three gerunds.

_____

_____ favorite summer pastimes.

6. Complete the sentence using gerund phrases.

Singing in the shower, _____ , and

_____—that's how my brother relaxes.

7. Complete the sentence using action words with direct objects.

I peeled the potatoes, _____ , and

_____ .

Extend: Watch for parallel structure in everything you read. Copy especially fine parallel sentences into a notebook or computer folder. Try writing sentences with similar constructions.

© Houghton Mifflin Harcourt Publishing Company

TEKS 9.17C
ELPS 4C, 5E

Review: Sentence Problems 2

> **Rewrite** the sentences below to correct the following problems: deadwood and wordiness, dangling or misplaced modifiers, nonstandard language, and unparallel construction.

1. Looking more confused than ever, Mr. Brown told Michael to come in during study hall for help.

_____

_____

_____

2. Trent tried to sell a set of clubs to beginning golfers with oversized heads.

_____

_____

_____

3. I could of made it to the movie on time if my tire hadn't of gone flat.

_____

_____

_____

4. The night was filled with the howls of unknown beasts, with moaning winds, and the shadows were dark and menacing.

_____

_____

_____

5. While moving the couch, the dog ran out the door and down the street.

_____

_____

_____

© Houghton Mifflin Harcourt Publishing Company

 **TEKS** 9.13C, 9.17C
ELPS 4C, 5E

6. Chasing the dog with her hair in a ponytail, Marta raced down the street.

_____

_____

_____

7. They should have tried harder to get here on time and left earlier and called us when they realized they were going to be late and had more consideration.

_____

_____

_____

8. We rode our bikes to the post office and to the store, and then our bikes were ridden off to the park.

_____

_____

_____

9. By the time we were through chopping firewood, we had nearly chopped a full cord of wood.

_____

_____

_____

10. My brother's room is full of half-eaten sandwiches, empty water bottles, and laying all over the place are dirty clothes.

_____

_____

_____

© Houghton Mifflin Harcourt Publishing Company

ELPS 4C

Pretest: Shifts in Construction

Shifts in construction may occur in four different ways: number (changing from singular to plural or vice versa), tense (mixing present, past, and future tenses), person (mixing 1st, 2nd, and 3rd persons), or voice (mixing active and passive voice).

> **Write** the correction above the second underlined part in each sentence. The underlined words in the following sentences show incorrect shifts in construction.

1. When <u>you</u> know it wasn't your fault, it is hard for *you* <u>one</u> to apologize.

2. Resisting <u>your</u> classmate's invitation to skip out may be the first step toward improving <u>one's</u> self-image.

3. Momentarily escaping their trainer, the circus elephants <u>headed</u> down the street, single file and trunk to tail, just as they <u>are</u> taught.

4. The oil riggers <u>drilled</u> deep under the ocean floor and <u>were watching</u> as a column of saltwater and sand sprayed high in the air.

5. Janelle <u>will sculpt</u> the clay carefully so that it <u>had</u> all the details of the original.

6. The <u>archaeologists</u> are looking for pottery that will give <u>him</u> clues about how the natives prepared food.

7. Swooping from its nest on the cliff, the bald eagle <u>snatched</u> its eaglet in midair, just before it <u>hits</u> the ground.

8. The weather last week was incredible—major snowstorms <u>hit</u> the Midwest and tornadoes <u>had been hitting</u> the South.

9. If the skateboard park were built, then the <u>boarders</u> would have a place to practice <u>his or her</u> techniques.

10. When <u>they</u> told you they were going to be here "in a little while," <u>she</u> should have been more specific.

11. The large raccoon <u>poked</u> his masked face into the garbage can while three little "masqueraders" <u>were watching</u> intently.

© Houghton Mifflin Harcourt Publishing Company

★ ELPS 4C, 5E

Shifts in Construction

A *shift in construction* is a change in the structure or style midway through a sentence. These shifts can occur in number, tense, person, or voice. For more information about agreement see pages 794, 796, and 798 in *Write Source*.

> **Study** the underlined shifts in number, tense, person, or voice in the following sentences. You may cross out words and write in new ones as necessary to correct the shifts. See the first sentence to understand how some of the sentences can be corrected in more than one way.

1. Before a driver backs out of a driveway, they should make sure that the road is
she or he
clear.

(or) Before a driver backs out of a driveway, they should make sure that the road is
drivers back
clear.

2. If you cannot finish painting the house before winter, one should wait until spring to start.

3. Because Lauren waited for just the right moment, many opportunities were missed by her.

4. In the story, Zenon stole a load of manure; then he starts feeling guilty—and smelly.

5. The Masked Marvel saved a busload of students in the morning, and a planeload of senior citizens were rescued by him in the afternoon.

6. One should refrain from speaking if you cannot control your temper.

7. The next person to walk through the door will become our secretary if they can write legibly.

8. Renaldo tested over a dozen boom boxes before he will buy just the right one.

9. Make sure that each of you has a full set of stakes for their tent.

10. Why does everyone think that they are the absolute center of the universe?

Extend: Use the following indefinite pronouns in compound or complex sentences: *someone, everything, neither*. Make sure your sentences do not contain a shift in number.

© Houghton Mifflin Harcourt Publishing Company

ELPS 4C, 5B

Shifts in Verb Tense 1

Consistent verb tenses clearly establish time in sentences. When verb tenses change without warning or for no reason, readers become confused. Turn to 762.3–764 in *Write Source* for information about the six different "times" that verb tenses communicate to the reader.

> **Underline** the verb in the first sentence of each pair. Change the verb tense in the second sentence to be consistent with the first. Finally, identify the tense that is used.

present **1.** Sicily is a small island off the tip of Italy. It ~~was~~ *is* about the size of New Hampshire.

_____ **2.** Mountains and hills cover more than 85 percent of Sicily. Mount Etna, a snowcapped volcano, will be the highest peak.

_____ **3.** In the fifth century B.C.E., the Greeks controlled the island. By the end of the century, the Carthaginians had challenged the Greeks for control.

_____ **4.** A few centuries later, Rome gained control over the island. After years of wars, Sicily finally had become part of Italy in 1860.

_____ **5.** Sicily's industries produce ships and refine petroleum. Tuna and other kinds of fishing have dominated the coastal economy.

_____ **6.** About one-fourth of the Sicilians work in agriculture. Retailing, service industries, and civil service occupations will have accounted for about half the island's income.

_____ **7.** Workers commute daily by ferry from Messina, Sicily's main seaport, to the Italian mainland. A lack of jobs in Sicily made this necessary.

_____ **8.** Sicily is the largest and most populous island in the Mediterranean. Sicilians have been enjoying a moderate climate.

Extend: Tell why the tense used for each pair of sentences is appropriate. For example, the present tense is appropriate in the first sentence because it speaks of a state of being that exists right now. Use the information about verb tenses on 762.3–764 in *Write Source* to help you with this activity.

© Houghton Mifflin Harcourt Publishing Company

Shifts in Verb Tense 2

In most cases, writers use the same verb tense throughout a sentence, a paragraph, or an entire piece of writing. Maintaining verb-tense consistency establishes the time of the actions being described. Readers know "what happened when" and are not confused. Turn to 762.3–764 in *Write Source*.

> **Underline** the first verb in the sentences below. Then change the other verbs to match the tense of the first verb.

1. Ultrasonics is the study of sound waves that ~~occurred~~ *occur* above our hearing capacity; today ultrasonics ~~was~~ *is* used in a variety of different ways.

2. In the early 1900s, ultrasound was a novelty, but by 1930, ultrasonics will become an important field of study.

3. Beginning in the 1960s, ultrasonic devices were used to detect flaws in metals, wood, and other materials, and the devices also start to replace the use of X-rays.

4. Ultrasonic waves are able to detect objects that did not transmit light, so they were used to find objects underwater.

5. This process is called *sonar*. Sonar identified submarines, has mapped the ocean bottom, and will measure the thickness of ice packs.

6. Ultrasonic devices have many medical applications; these included using ultrasound to shatter kidney stones and gallstones.

7. Today, ultrasound's primary medical use is the procedure called *imaging*, in which ultrasonic waves were used to create images of internal body structures or monitor tumors, cysts, and even fetuses.

8. Imaging is a painless process and took only a few short minutes to complete.

9. Doctors diagnose diseases and will evaluate internal organs using ultrasound.

Extend: Read a section of a history textbook. Identify the tense of the verbs. Does the book's use of tense create a clear picture for you?

© Houghton Mifflin Harcourt Publishing Company

ELPS 4C

Pronoun Shifts

Pronoun shifts occur when a writer "shifts" from using a singular pronoun to a plural pronoun or vice versa, from a masculine pronoun to a feminine pronoun or vice versa, and from a neutral-gender pronoun to a masculine or feminine pronoun or vice versa. Turn to 754.1 and 754.2, 756.2 and 798.2 in *Write Source*.

> **Circle** the correct pronoun in the following sentences.

1. My grandparents seem to like *(his and her, their)* new surround-sound system.

2. My grandpa especially likes *(his, their)* personal remote headset.

3. Grandpa now thinks that everyone should have *(his or her, their)* own headset.

4. My grandma likes to listen to *(her, their)* radio program while grandpa watches his game shows.

5. Both can watch or listen to whatever *(he or she, they)* want.

> **Cross out** pronoun shifts in the following passage and write the correct pronoun above. Remember to be consistent throughout the passage. You may also need to change the number of some verbs.

1   Teenagers everywhere have favorite activities and favorite foods, but in

2   Hawaii ~~he or she has~~ *they have* some that are quite different. In Hawaii teens often learn

3   to use surfboards or body boards. On the surfboard, you stand up; and on the

4   body board, one lies down. Some teens learn the hula, an ancient Hawaiian

5   dance. Hula dancers use her or his hands to tell a story while moving her legs

6   and hips. And Hawaiian teens often learn how to snow ski. Yes, he or she can

7   ski in Hawaii! It snows at the top of Mauna Kea during the winter. All this

8   activity makes them hungry, and in Hawaii when you order fast food, one gets

9   burgers, fries, and shakes as well as Portuguese sausages and Hawaiian noodle

10   soup. Hawaii sounds like a great place to live.

© Houghton Mifflin Harcourt Publishing Company

ELPS 4C

Review: Shifts in Construction

> **Cross out** shifts in the following sentences and write the corrections, if necessary, above. Watch for shifts in person, voice, number, and verb tense.

1. Darrick called the grocery store to see if it has closed for the night.

2. The photographers shot several pictures of cheetahs, antelopes, and zebras, but he saw no lions.

3. She walked through the refuge, and they observed the damage caused by the broken dam.

4. Tara is working in Department 307 but hoped to be transferred soon.

5. People who look on the bright side in a bad situation are the one you generally want to be with when things go wrong.

6. I was ready to leave at 9:30, but then I get a phone call.

7. We visited the museum, we saw the dinosaurs, and then souvenirs were bought.

8. Each person must sign the application form, or they will not be admitted.

9. Nutritious food gives a person energy, and a good night's sleep produced a positive attitude.

10. The chipmunks raced across the park and will fight over the spilled bag of popcorn.

11. Howling winds from the north swept over the tiny cabin and swirl the snow into giant drifts.

12. Dad bought tickets, so we took the train and the fall scenery was viewed with excitement.

© Houghton Mifflin Harcourt Publishing Company

ELPS 4C

Review: Sentence Activities

> **Complete** the following statements.

1. A(n) _____ is the error of connecting two simple sentences with only a comma.

2. A(n) _____ sentence is one that seems to go on and on.

3. A(n) _____ modifier is one that is placed too far away from the word it modifies in the sentence.

4. A(n) _____ happens when two sentences run together without punctuation or connecting words.

5. _____ is wording that fills up lots of space but does not add anything important or new to the overall meaning.

6. A sentence _____ is a group of words that is not a complete sentence.

7. In the sentence *There goes a magnificent specimen of humankind,* the simple subject is _____ .

8. _____ is the repeating of phrases or sentences that are similar in structure.

9. _____ modifiers appear to modify the wrong word or a word that isn't in the sentence.

10. A complete sentence must have a(n) _____ and a(n) _____ and express a complete thought.

11. A(n) _____ sentence postpones the crucial or most surprising idea until the end.

12. In the sentence *Can you guess my age?,* the simple predicate is _____ .

© Houghton Mifflin Harcourt Publishing Company

ELPS 4C

13. A(n) _____ sentence contains two simple sentences joined by a semicolon or by a comma with a(n) _____ .

14. Sentences make five different kinds of statements: declarative, _____ , _____ , _____ , or conditional.

15. In the sentence *Mr. Kotter, my favorite teacher, is back,* the phrase *my favorite teacher* is a(n) _____ .

16. *Why do I bother?* is what kind of sentence? _____

17. Sentences have four different basic structures: simple, _____ , _____ , and _____ .

18. A pronoun must agree with its antecedent in _____ , _____ , and _____ .

19. A(n) _____ sentence contains one independent clause and one or more dependent clauses.

20. _____ sentences give commands.

21. The three basic types of subordinate clauses are _____ , _____ , and _____ .

22. The subject and verb of any clause must agree in both _____ and _____ .

23. *Team, crowd,* and *pair* are _____ nouns; whether they take a singular or a plural verb depends on how they are used.

24. Sentences can be combined in the following ways: by using _____ , _____ , _____ , _____ , _____ , _____ , _____ , _____ .

© Houghton Mifflin Harcourt Publishing Company